Tantalus and the Pelican

Exploring Monastic Spirituality Today

NICHOLAS BUXTON

continuum

Continuum International Publishing Group

The Tower Building   80 Maiden Lane

11 York Road   Suite 704

London   New York

SE1 7NX   NY 10038

www.continuumbooks.com

First published 2009

British Library Cataloguing-in-Publication Data
A catalogue record for this book is available from the British Library.

ISBN 9781847061119

Typeset by Newgen Imaging Systems Pvt Ltd, Chennai, India
Printed and bound by MPG Books, Cornwall

Contents

Acknowledgements

This book is dedicated to all the monks and nuns I have known over the years, and the various religious communities around the world that I have visited or stayed at. Without them, none of this would ever have happened.

Particular thanks are also due to the many friends who read or discussed work in progress, at any stage from the initial proposal through to completion of the final manuscript, especially: Joel Cabrita, Catherine Clarke, Benedicta Ward, Robin Baird-Smith, Richard Lock-Pullan, Jenny Hancock, Ernest Lennon, Robin Davis, Crispin Hay, Joanna Jepson, Luke Jolly, Stephen Hearn, Venetia Bridges, David Stevenson, Cyril Pierce and Marie-Claire Lucas. Their comments and suggestions have been invaluable, undoubtedly making this a better book than it otherwise would have been.

Introduction

The first time I stayed in a monastery I thought it was one of the most exciting things I had ever done. The passage of time has done nothing to dampen my initial enthusiasm, and years later I still get a buzz from the rarefied atmosphere of religious communities. Strange as it might seem in this supposedly secular age, many are fascinated by the monastic life – though they may otherwise have little interest in the church. Indeed, people frequently say they can see why being in a monastery might be appealing – all that peace and quiet, nice countryside, time to read and take leisurely walks – but they wouldn't be able to buy into the whole 'God' bit. What this usually means is that they are interested in spirituality – generally understood in terms of a personal quest for healing and wholeness – as long as it does not have anything to do with religion, which is perceived as being irrevocably bound up with irrational beliefs, meaningless rituals and irrelevant institutions. But 'spirituality' is a notoriously slippery word. For religious people, it is an essential part of being religious; for almost everybody else, it is the antithesis of religion. In theory, it is all about our search for meaning and fulfilment; in practice, we are more likely to come across it as a marketing strategy or a popular fad.

TANTALUS AND THE PELICAN

It is often supposed that 'genuine' religion – in other words, spirituality – is defined by interior experiences; a personal relationship with the divine, conducted largely, as it also turns out, on terms one decides for oneself. What this private faith lacks, however, is any notion of public accountability. By contrast, what I have discovered – primarily from staying in monasteries – is that to be religious (or spiritual for that matter, for you cannot have one without the other), to be most fully who and what we really are, is to be formed and defined by relationship to a shared story, and to engage with and participate in a collective practice. Rather than seeing spirituality and religion as separate – or worse, as opposed – I suggest that if spirituality refers to the innate human instinct to seek meaning and fulfilment, then religion is the formalization of that in terms of a way of life, to which we have a duty to be faithful and true. Thus religion and spirituality are inseparable: if you divorce one from the other it becomes either vacuous or lifeless.

In what follows, I am going to be talking a lot about monks and monking. This is not to say that everybody should join a monastery, nor that monks and nuns are somehow better than other people. They are not always holy and certainly not perfect. In fact they are just like you and me: typical, imperfect human beings trying to find meaning and fulfilment, trying to live decent and peaceful lives. They just do it more deliberately. And this is precisely why there is something we can all learn from the monastic life, whoever we are: male or female, committed to faith or agnostic. Even though we may have no intention of following them into the cloister, there are nevertheless many ways in which we can benefit by imitating their inspiring example.

CHAPTER ONE

INTO THE DESERT

Tradition has it that Christian monasticism emerged in the deserts of Egypt during the third century, but the truth is nobody really knows quite how or why – or even where and when – as there is evidence for similar things happening in other parts of the eastern Roman empire during the same period. Some scholars have speculated that the first monks may simply have been men and women forced into poverty by the crushing burden of Roman taxation, or else fleeing the threat of persecution. Others suggest that in fact it was the ending of the great persecution of the Emperor Diocletian in 311, and thus the lack of further opportunities for martyrdom, that led some zealous Christians to seek other ways of giving up their life for Christ.

Monks themselves have always understood monasticism as 'life according to the Gospel', and it does not seem unreasonable to suppose that the people we now call 'monastic' were just trying to imitate the example of the first disciples, at a time when the church was becoming an increasingly institutionalized part of the establishment. After all, for the first three hundred years of its existence Christianity was a deviant sect, clinging precariously to the margins of society, its followers branded 'atheists' for their refusal to worship the gods of the state. Following Constantine's Edict of Milan in 313, however, Christians were for the first time free to practise their religion openly, and by the end of the century Christianity had become the official and only religion of the empire. In such circumstances it seems plausible to suggest that some Christians may have sought a return to the radically countercultural spirit of the early church, as envisaged in the Acts of the Apostles.[1]

Of course, the other thing we ought to remember is that monasticism is not a uniquely Christian phenomenon. There were undoubtedly religious communities in the region of the eastern Mediterranean long before the advent of Christianity; to say nothing of the foundation of Buddhist monasticism in India five centuries before the birth of Christ. These facts would seem to suggest that human beings simply have a perennial and universal urge to renounce the world and seek God: it is just something that some people feel the need to do, and what we call 'monasticism' is one of the various ways this has been expressed. However, this also means that it is virtually impossible to account for the specific historical causes and conditions that gave rise to the particular phenomenon of Christian monasticism in the deserts of Egypt, Syria and Palestine towards the end of the third century. What eventually emerged in the form we now recognize as 'monastic' was part of a diffuse web of wider religious and cultural trends, each with long and complex histories.

Although the precise origins of monasticism may be unclear, we do have a wealth of literature – including sayings and anecdotes, travellers' tales, letters, and biographies – that provide us with a rich source of information about the life and thought of early Egyptian

---

[1] For example: 'All who believed were together and had all things in common' (Acts 2.44, Cf. 4.32).

monasticism during its heyday in the fourth century. Of these, perhaps the best-known today are the collections of pithy sayings attributed to the so-called 'Desert Fathers', which usually recall a conversation between master and disciple, or an example of edifying (and frequently unconventional) behaviour. Thus, they are not theological discourses as such, but practical words of wisdom, born from deep experience of the spiritual life – often arising from a question put to a monk or the characteristic request, 'give me a word'. Initially these sayings would have circulated orally, before being arranged and written down in their present form in the fifth or sixth century. Various compilations have survived: two of the best-known being the 'Alphabetical Collection' and the 'Systematic Collection'.[2]

In addition there are the histories, which consist of anecdotes and biographies of desert monks, and include the anonymous *Historia Monachorum in Aegypto* and the *Lausiac History* of Palladius. The former purports to be the account of a journey through Egypt undertaken by the un-named author and six companions during the course of several months between 394 and 395. In the prologue the author states his intention to write an 'account of the practices of the Egyptian monks which I have witnessed, their fervent love and great discipline'.[3] The latter, written by Palladius (c. 363–431), in about 420, consists primarily of some seventy portraits of the monks of

---

[2] Extracts from the Alphabetical Collection taken from: Benedicta Ward (trans.), *The Sayings of the Desert Fathers: The Alphabetical Collection* (Kalamazoo: Cistercian Publications, 1975). Extracts from the Systematic Collection taken from: Benedicta Ward (trans.), *The Desert Fathers: Sayings of the Early Christian Monks* (London: Penguin Books, 2003).

[3] Norman Russell (trans.), *The Lives of the Desert Fathers* (London: Mowbray, 1981), p. 49.

Nitria and Kellia, as well as some ascetics of other lands, and – interestingly – quite a number of women, 'so that no one could plead as an excuse that women are too weak to practise virtue successfully'.[4]

Whatever the reason – whether motivated by an ardent hope for the imminent return of Christ, or just fleeing a world gone mad – the fact is that large numbers of men and women turned their backs on society in order to seek God and follow the teachings of Jesus as completely as possible. Such was the popularity of this movement that according to some reports there were thousands of men and women leading a monastic life, both in towns and out in the desert, making the latter into a 'heavenly city' on account of the number of hermits living there. The author of the *Historia Monachorum* cites some impressive numbers: Abba Or headed a monastery of one thousand monks, Ammon was spiritual father to three thousand, while Abba Sarapion was the superior of an enormous community of ten thousand.[5] In a description of the city of Oxyrhynchus we are told there were twelve churches, with five thousand monks living within the city and as many again outside it – a total that almost outnumbered the non-monastic population. Indeed the city was said to be 'so full of monasteries that the very walls resound with the voices of the monks'.[6] Even if these figures are exaggerated, we can nevertheless be certain that by the early fourth century the term *monachos* (monk) was in common usage, as an Egyptian papyrus dated to 324 confirms.

---

[4] Robert Meyer (trans.), *Palladius: The Lausiac History* (New York: Paulist Press, 1964), p. 117.

[5] Russell, *Lives*, pp. 63, 65 and 102.

[6] Ibid., p. 67.

There was one book, however, which did more than any other to promote the archetype of the monastic hero. Indeed it was to become the inspiration for a whole new literary genre: hagiography – the life of a saint. Written in about 357 by Athanasius, Patriarch of Alexandria, the *Life of Antony* very rapidly became one of the most popular and influential books in the Christian world; a fact confirmed by no less a figure than Augustine of Hippo, who finally made up his mind to become a Christian as a result of it. Athanasius maintains that he knew Antony personally – claiming to have met him often – yet the Antony we read about in the pages of the *Life* seems to be a very different person from the Antony we encounter in the letters attributed to him, or the sayings recorded under his name. Whether he really knew Antony or not, there can be little doubt that Athanasius was acquainted with the monks of the desert, as he is known to have spent the third of his five periods of exile – from 356 to 362 – in hiding among them, and it is during this time that he wrote the *Life*. Therefore, even if the *Life* tell us more about Athanasius and his theological concerns than it does about Antony, this in no way detracts from its significance. Athanasius sets out to explain and illustrate the principles of the monastic life. Judging by the reception of his book, he clearly succeeded.

Commonly – if improbably – known as the first monk, Antony (c. 254–356), was the son of well-to-do and devout parents who died when he was about eighteen or twenty, leaving him in charge of the family farm. One day, barely six months later, he was walking to church thinking about how the apostles had given up everything to follow Jesus. He arrived just in time to hear the reading from Matthew's gospel in which a young man comes to Jesus and says: 'Teacher, what good deed must I do to have eternal life?' To my mind, this is a question about freedom, because to have 'eternal life' would mean being free of everything that limits us, symbolized by the ultimate limit that is death. The answer Jesus gives may not be what we expect. 'If you wish to be perfect, go, sell your possessions, and give the money to the poor, and you will have treasure in heaven; then come, follow me.'[7] Note that he does not say, 'If you want to go to heaven when you die, then sell all your belongings.' He says that if you want to be *perfect* – or most fully what you truly are – then free yourself of your attachments. Evidently this was not what the rich young man who asked the question wanted to hear. The story continues: 'When the young man heard this word, he went away grieving, for he had many possessions.' Freedom – contrary to what advertisers would have us believe – is not necessarily the outcome of having enough money to be able to do whatever we want. Quite the opposite, in fact. Wealth – which here refers not only to material goods but whatever we invest with value – is more likely to inhibit our freedom and make us its slave. To invest our 'treasure' in 'heaven', by contrast, is to identify with what really matters, that which is not transient but eternal.

The story of the rich young man had a profound and moving effect on me one day as I heard it being read while I was staying in a monastery. At the time, I was thinking long and hard about what I should be doing in life, and how best to become the person I was really meant to be. I was also thinking about whether or not I might have a vocation to the religious life. Suddenly – and for the first time – I realized with a heartbreaking pang that I was the rich young man.

---

[7] Matthew 19.16–22.

We all are in one way or another. I may not have a lot of money, but I do 'own' much that is valuable to me, such as my desires to enjoy and experience life, the skills and talents I possess, the things I have achieved or still wish to accomplish, and so on. Like the rich young man, I am unable to give up the things to which I am most attached – in which, to be more precise, my sense of identity is most heavily invested – and therefore I am unable to do that which in my heart of hearts I know to be what really matters. Having caught a glimpse of freedom, but unable to pay the price, I too turned away with tears in my eyes.

Antony, however, was made of sterner stuff. Feeling personally spoken to by the word of God in holy scripture – 'as if the passage were read on his account'[8] – he gave away the family property, sold his possessions, and donated the proceeds to the poor – keeping back just enough for the maintenance of his younger sister. At a later date, he heard another reading – this time from the Sermon on the Mount – in which Jesus says 'do not worry about tomorrow'.[9] Needing no further encouragement, Antony gave away what little still remained, packed his little sister off to a nunnery, and dedicated himself from then onwards to the spiritual life. Initially he remained close to home, learning what he could from local ascetics and imitating their example. Over time he gradually withdrew further and further from the world, in order that he might endeavour to 'pray without ceasing'. At about the age of thirty-five he moved deeper

---

[8] Robert Gregg (trans.), *Athanasius: The Life of Antony and The Letter to Marcellinus* (New York: Paulist Press, 1980), p. 31.
[9] Matthew 6.34.

into the desert and barricaded himself inside an abandoned fort. As his fame spread, he began to acquire quite a following: hordes of pilgrims came to the fort and camped outside, hoping for a few words of spiritual instruction, or even just a glimpse of the revered holy man. Feeling the need for even greater solitude, he set off into the desert once more, and after three days found himself at the 'Inner Mountain'. To this day, the monastery named after him stands at the foot of the mountainside; halfway up it is the cave where he spent the remaining forty years of his long life.

Broadly speaking, monasticism has taken two principal forms – solitary and communal – though we should be wary of trying to distinguish too sharply between them. Monks who live together are still living apart from the rest of society, thus in a kind of solitude; and even solitaries congregate for acts of public worship. One way or another then, monasticism involves both a flight from the world, and the creation of alternative communities – workshops of the spiritual life – structured in such a way as to provide the conditions most conducive to the search for God. Nevertheless, in as much as we can make this slightly artificial distinction between two streams, Antony is usually held to be the exemplar of and primary inspiration for the eremitic tradition of the desert fathers. It is from this term, derived from *eremos* (the Greek word for a desert), that we also get the English word 'hermit'. The desert fathers were men – and some women too – who, conscious of their mortal limitations, or 'sin', withdrew to the barren wilderness of the empty desert in order to be with God in solitude and silence. Living either in caves or simple cells made from mud bricks, sometimes far from others, but more often clustered together, they spent their days in prayer, fasting, recitation of the psalms, and manual labour – especially basket-weaving and rope-plaiting. This was no easy life. The desert is an extremely hostile environment, altogether unfit for human habitation.

One of the most famous of these monastic settlements was Scetis, founded by Macarius the Great (c. 300–390) – a former camel trader and sometime smuggler – in about 330. Before settling at Scetis, Macarius had been falsely accused of getting a young woman pregnant. Instead of denying the charge, however, he simply made more baskets in order that he might be able to support his new 'wife'. When the woman went into labour, she was unable to give birth until finally she confessed that Macarius was not in fact the father. Upon learning the truth, the villagers went to offer Macarius their homage and apologies, but not wishing to be the centre of attention he left town and made his home in the wilderness. Now less than two hours by car from Cairo, Scetis (also known as Wadi Natrun) was, in the fourth century, an inhospitable marshy area, lacking good drinking water. It took a day and a half to get there, and – due to the absence of roads – was impossible to find unless one could navigate by the stars. The significance of this last point should not be underestimated: getting lost in the desert could be fatal.

Macarius, nicknamed the 'old young man' on account of his reputation for wisdom beyond his years, was a colourful character who attracted a large circle of disciples. On one occasion, he returned to his cell to find a man stealing his (presumably few) possessions and loading them up onto his donkey. Instead of rebuking the thief, however, Macarius calmly helped him finish packing before cheerfully seeing him on his way with a quotation from the Bible: 'We brought nothing into the world, so that we can take nothing out of it.'[10]

Ironically, although they retreated from society in order to be alone before God, the monks of the Egyptian desert were, and indeed still are, joined in their solitude by noisy crowds of visitors, seeking blessings from them on account of their reputation for holiness and the widely held belief that they possessed supernatural powers. Whether supernatural or not, there can be little doubt that by culti-vating detachment from self-interest, the ascetic acquires a very real power the rest of us do not have. People in authority, for example, can have little control over someone who has removed themselves from the socio-economic structures by which the rest of us are bound. After all, there are no sanctions you can impose on someone who has already renounced the world. It may seem improbable at first, but an ascetic's power derives from their humility: with nothing to lose, they become invulnerable, and thus potentially threatening to the 'authorities'. Indeed, the desert hermits were quite literally untouch-able. On one occasion, we are told, a demon was trying to attack Macarius with a sickle, but could not so much as even scratch him. The demon complains that although he can go without food or sleep, outdoing Macarius in all his ascetic practices, there is one thing he cannot match: humility. For that reason, the demon was unable to prevail against him.[11]

This brings us to another important aspect of what is sometimes rather cosily referred to as 'desert spirituality'. The early monks not

---

[10] 1 Timothy 6.7.
[11] *Alphabetical Collection* Macarius 11.

only had to cope with the unforgiving physical elements, they also had to engage in a battle of wills with elemental forces of another kind, as the desert was believed to be infested with demons, sometimes equated with the pagan deities who had been driven from the cities by the triumph of Christianity. For this reason the path of purification is invariably characterized in terms of struggling against and overcoming the onslaughts of demonic forces. But how should we actually understand this talk of 'demons'? On the one hand, it would seem that demons were believed to be real entities; that is, evil spirits inhabiting living bodies in whom they manifested the various sins of anger, greed, pride, vanity, lustful obsessions, and so on. On the other hand, the desert fathers do sometimes seem to suggest that demons might be a manifestation of what we would probably call 'egotism', implying that even – or indeed especially – in the literature of early monasticism, demons could be understood in ways that we would now describe as 'psychological'. According to a saying attributed to Abba Poemen, one of the most oft-quoted desert fathers, 'when we follow our self-will then our wills seem like demons'.[12] It is not so hard to see how we might relate this to our own everyday experience. For example, I have found that if I cut myself off from whatever normally fills my life and engages my attention – such as by going on retreat to the artificial desert of a monastery – then my imagination will be swamped by obsessive and uncontrollable fantasies and anxieties. Left alone with nothing but itself, the mind desperately tries to compensate for the lack of its customary diet of thoughts and activities: all the things that usually – and quite literally – *possess* my mind.

---

[12] *Systematic Collection* Discretion 62.

11

The solitary life could thus be fraught with danger, both physical and mental. As well as the basic challenge of surviving under the most severe conditions, the desert hermit had to contend with their demons (whatever we might understand by that), and the treacherous pitfalls of self-delusion. Even in everyday life, we all know how easy it can be to lose the plot or otherwise get carried away – either with enthusiasm or anxiety – if our friends do not keep us grounded. On top of that, there is a further problem confronting the Christian who chooses to live alone: how are they to fulfil the Gospel injunction to love their neighbour? Some early church fathers – most notably Basil of Caesarea (c. 330–379) – concluded that the fullest expression of religious life was to be found not in a flight from the world, but community. In the late 350s, Basil established a rural retreat in Pontus (which today would be in northern Turkey), with his friend Gregory of Nazianzus. Here they studied the writings of the great Alexandrian theologian Origen, and formulated a monastic ideal based on charitable works. It is in no small part due to Basil's influence that religious orders came to be involved in running schools and hospitals, and promoting scholarship and the arts.

Some of the very first formally constituted monasteries were founded during the 320s by Antony's younger contemporary Pachomius (c. 292–346), author of the earliest known monastic rule. Pagan by birth, Pachomius was conscripted into the army in 312–313. While his company was billeted at Thebes, he was so impressed by the kindness and generosity of the Christians he encountered there that he decided to pray to their God, resolving that when he was released from the army, he would follow their example by devoting himself to a life of service. On the eve of his baptism he had a vision of dew falling from heaven and spilling into his hand as honey, which then spread over the earth. Taking this as a sign of his calling, he apprenticed himself to a hermit called Palamon. One day, when praying near the deserted village of Tabennesi, he heard a voice telling him to build a monastery there, which he duly did with his brother John. The two could not agree, however, about what kind of community it should be. John thought they should stick to the eremitic model; Pachomius felt inspired to do something on a much larger scale. Shortly thereafter, Pachomius had a further vision while out cutting reeds, this time of an angel who told him it was God's will that he should minister to the whole of humanity. Encouraged by this sign he expanded the community, accepting all who came to him wanting to follow the monastic life.

Pachomius founded several monasteries and convents in Upper Egypt: nine for men and two for women. These communities were highly regimented, with a well-defined organizational structure and orderly timetable, possibly reflecting his military background. Monks and nuns were required to eat, sleep, and work together – for the most part in silence – to dress identically, and keep to their allotted places at meals and at prayer. From what we can tell Pachomian monasteries contained several hundred monks, and were divided into houses of about twenty. At dawn they would rise for morning prayer – a service consisting of Bible readings and meditation – after which they would return to their cells to await instructions concerning the day's work. Divided into cohorts, the monks would be allocated their respective tasks, which would be completed in silence. These monasteries seem to have been largely self-sufficient. In addition to the traditional basket-making, mention is made of monks working as tailors, metalworkers, carpenters and smiths, as well as in various forms of agriculture and animal husbandry; although some of this diversity may have been a later development. At lunch-time they ate their main meal of the day, consisting of bread and cooked vegetables, again in strict silence. A light snack was provided in the evening, and it seems this may have been followed by a period of spiritual instruction or discussion, before night prayer and bed. This basic structure, albeit with some modifications, has remained more or less the standard template for monastic communities up until the present day. It provides a framework that is intended to nourish and sustain body and mind, and – most importantly – a mutually supportive environment conducive to seeking God.

Life in a Pachomian monastery may seem harsh by today's stand-ards, but it would not have been any tougher than the life of the average Egyptian peasant. Seen in context, it was actually relatively balanced, with little evidence of the excessive or competitive zeal for austerity that we might associate with the great ascetics of Syria – such as Simon of Stylite, who famously stood on top of a pillar for forty-seven years. There is a story that illustrates this point rather nicely. One day Macarius of Alexandria, a desert hermit famous for his asceticism (and not to be confused with Macarius the Great), went to Pachomius' monastery at Tabennesi disguised as a novice in order to verify the reports he had heard concerning the self-disci-pline of the monks there. Macarius easily outdid them all. Remaining without food, drink, or sleep for the whole of Lent, he provoked an outcry among the brethren, who could not possibly match his feats of abstinence. Discerning in a vision the stranger's true identity, Pachomius thanked Macarius for putting his young monks in their place and edifying them by his example, before politely asking him to leave.

What we learn from this story is that for Pachomius, self-knowledge was born of and resulted in a deep knowledge of others, as demonstrated by his reputed ability to 'read hearts'. This seemingly occult ability to know things about people they do not even know themselves is perhaps more readily associated with exotic tales of yogis, fakirs, and inscrutable Zen masters, yet the logic underlying it is fairly straightforward. After all, if the deepest truth of what we are is the ground of being we all share, then to know one's own self is to know the self of others also. This is why self-knowledge is sometimes likened to a knowledge of the clay from which all pots are made. Or, to put it another way, if everything that exists does so by virtue of its participation in the being of God, then to know the truth about God is to know the truth about everything. Such knowledge can, however, seem threatening to some people: Pachomius' ability to 'read hearts' resulted in his arraignment before an ecclesiastical court at Latopolis in 345.

I have to admit that my own interest in spirituality was, to begin with, at least partly stimulated by stories of such 'powers'. That, and the dawning realization that being human presents certain problems, to which – it is claimed – the practise of a spiritual discipline offers a solution.

CHAPTER TWO

Something More?

Shortly after God creates the world, something goes horribly wrong. The devil appears to Eve in the guise of a whispering serpent, tempting her to eat the forbidden fruit of the tree of the knowledge of good and evil, saying 'you will be like God'. She eats the fruit, Adam does likewise, and 'the eyes of both were opened'. When their disobedience is discovered, God curses the serpent and banishes Adam and Eve from paradise. In so doing he condemns them, and all their descendants, to a life of suffering. Sex and death enter the world.

This deceptively simple allegory functions as our primary foundational myth, explaining the problem of being human: the fact that we find ourselves in a condition of suffering and alienation. As such, it is the story that has shaped the world we live in. I'm not saying that is good or bad – it is just a fact. If it wasn't this particular story, it would be some other one. Human beings are mythological creatures: possessing what we call an imagination, we instinctively create stories that explain why things are – or are experienced to be – the way they are, and what we might be able to do about it. I have always been intrigued by such stories, whether from the Bible or Greek mythology, even though I did not have a particularly religious upbringing. That is to say, I went to chapel at school – because it was compulsory – and occasionally, rather reluctantly, attended carol services at Christmas. I must have had some sort of faith, however, because when the time came, it seemed natural that I should get confirmed.

In the Church of England – of which I was, by default, a member – this is typically the occasion when an individual, christened as a baby, elects to confirm the baptismal vows originally made on their behalf. It can also function, albeit weakly, as an archetypal rite of passage, a coming-of-age ritual symbolizing a person's transition from membership of a family to membership of the wider public community. It seems fitting therefore that it should take place at the age of puberty, that stage in our physical and psychological development when we change from a child into an adult, acquiring in the process a new awareness of ourselves as autonomous individuals.

During the course of the preparatory classes, however, I found myself reacting fiercely against everything I was being told. I am not quite sure exactly what put me off. Religious instruction often has an infuriating tendency to be childishly simplistic, when in reality things tend to be rather more complicated. I distinctly remember being presented with a picture of the supposedly ideal life – a happy family, a good job, a nice house, and so on – which I found totally suffocating. If this was what being a Christian was all about, then it wasn't for me. And so, thanks to the preparation I had received, by the time I was confirmed I was basically an atheist: actively hostile towards religion in general, and the church in particular, which seemed corrupt and hypocritical. Yet at the same time I burned with a passionate desire to seek truth. It mattered. I wanted to know what was what, and I wanted answers to the 'Big Questions'.

By coincidence, I started to find some of those answers in the teachings of Buddhism, according to which the whole of human existence is stained by an all-pervasive and deeply frustrating sense of unsatisfactoriness called *duhkha*. The notion that life is fraught with physical suffering should be obvious enough, but the Buddha also insisted that even pleasures leave us with *duhkha* once they have passed away. *Duhkha* is therefore based on another doctrine: that everything is impermanent. Seeing this for the first time struck me like the proverbial thunderbolt. Of course, nothing lasts. Nothing. Impermanence applies not only to objects, and states of mind, but also theoretical concepts, rules and statutes, social institutions, laws of nature, and cultural conventions. In the final analysis, *duhkha* results from the identification – or, more accurately, the misidentification – of our selves with things and experiences that are transitory and impermanent. This includes our material possessions, our constantly changing physical body, our achievements, memories, hopes and fears. Everything, in short, that we think of or identify with as I, me or mine.

In a flash I understood the provisional nature of all that is, together with a vague notion of the deeper implication that ultimately nothing is – or at least, is not as it seems. It was, in all respects, a spiritual awakening: an immediate and profound apprehension of the problem of being human, coupled with a strong urge to do something about it. Together these two factors represent the starting point for the search for meaning and fulfilment that people use the language of spirituality to describe. I was fourteen, a pupil in a fairly well-known English boarding school: one of those character-building places where the classroom takes second place to the rugby field, and getting beaten by the headmaster – six of the best – was considered a badge of honour. Fourteen is an interesting age. As well as becoming an atheist and discovering Buddhism – not to mention drugs, alcohol, and the opposite sex – I also started to challenge everything that I had up until that point accepted without question, and this gave me the exhilarating feeling that I had suddenly woken up and begun to think for myself.

The fact that human beings can think at all is something we take for granted most of the time, although it should give us pause for thought. It suggests that we are creatures who have self-awareness, which is to say we have a fundamental intuition of being, an awareness of the irreducible fact of existence that some people call God. Whether we wish to say that God is the ground of Being, or that the ground of Being is what we call God, the important point is that we know that we are. At the same time, however, to be aware that we are logically entails being aware that we might not be, just as the self only is what it is in relation to that which is other than self. Self-awareness is thus the capacity to see ourselves and what we do objectively. This has two important consequences, which bear directly on the search for meaning on the one hand, and fulfilment on the other. The first is that we inevitably create stories in order to explain life and our relationship to the world, for to be aware of oneself as a knowing subject in relation to a known object implies also an account of that relationship: it is to posit a meaning of things in addition to the bare fact of the awareness of things. The second is that we have the capacity to imagine ourselves and our circumstances being different from the way they actually are. Indeed, much of our time is spent actively wishing for this to be the case, for things to be other than as they are.

To be self-aware is to attribute significance to our actions. In other words, we cannot just 'do' or 'be', like sheep wandering aimlessly across a field, with no sense of where we are going or why. Instead we must necessarily have some notion of a reason or purpose to account for the experience of what we are doing, and this is already the basis of a rudimentary story. When you take all these stories together you get what we call 'culture', our collective self-awareness, the shared objectification of ourselves as a society. Another word we could use to describe this collective self-awareness might be 'religion'; that is, our story about who we are, why we are here, and what we ought to do about it. This is not to dismiss religious belief as no more than a crutch to help certain credulous or needy individuals cope with the difficulties of life. It is rather that telling stories in order to create a meaningful world is simply something that human beings automatically do, and the word most commonly used to signify this activity is religion. To be religious, then, is a fact about being human, and as basic to us as being artistic, scientific, or political.

Even if we do not actively subscribe to an explicitly religious belief system, we still live our lives according to and within stories, be they grand sweeping narratives of universal meaning and purpose, the soap operas we watch on television, or merely the ordinary commerce of everyday social interaction. Thus it is not only religious people who tell stories about the world, what it means to be human, and how most fully to become that. We all do it, all the time. 'What's the story?' we say, when asking the explanation for something.

Story-telling is what we do because we are human: it is what makes us human, and it is how we express, signify, and comprehend what it means to be human. Just listen to any conversation, however mundane it might be, and you will notice that it consists almost entirely of story-telling. Listen closely and you will also discover that these stories come in only two genres: history and fantasy. One way or another, all our conversations involve either reconstructing events that have happened in the past or speculating about things that might happen in the future. Everything we say, hear, and see, is presented to us as some kind of a story, told from a particular perspective, and in order to convey a particular meaning.

The supposedly distinct boundary between truth and fiction now seems blurred at best, if not ultimately non-existent. It is all stories. This is not to say that religious stories are *merely* stories, in comparison with something else that is *really* true. I mean there are *only* stories. The very basis of human understanding itself, and not just the understanding of being human, is dependent upon such stories: there is no other way of being what we are. We inhabit a mythic universe, one that is imbued with human meaning; the world we experience is determined by our prior assumptions – or beliefs – concerning it. Whatever meaning our existence has, it is given by *us*, and that – whatever that story might be – is our way of making sense out of nonsense. We live in and according to stories, though we do not always see them as such because the story we are living in at any given time is always the story we call 'The Truth'. It is meaningless to ask what is outside the story, or what is *ultimately* true – there are only more stories. Faced by the purposelessness of the universe, and the meaninglessness of death, I make that fearful leap into the darkness of faith. Not because I am 'religious' – as if that were but one of the optional ways of being human – but because this is simply what it is to be human in the first place. In doing so, I act *as if* there is a reason for the fact that things are; that the story has a meaning; and that there is a point to it all.

Not everybody sees things this way, of course. Most people I know seem pretty sure about the difference between truth and fiction, and what is more, feel that religion in any form is simply irrelevant to them. Either they have an alternative and supposedly 'non-religious' belief system, or else life is going well enough as it is and they do not need any help from God. But when you think about it, this is an odd stance to take. I do not know many people who could honestly say they are perfectly happy with the way things are, and would not want to change anything about themselves or their circumstances. The desert fathers defined a monk as someone who 'makes himself content with just what he needs and no more'.[13] We, by contrast, are rarely satisfied with just what we need or what we have; if we were then we would not be constantly trying to be or become something other than what we already are. If we are not content, could it be possible that our striving for fulfilment might conceal a profound lack of something, something that our worldly aspirations cannot but fail to deliver?

So we seek. We seek for the satisfaction of our desires, be they material, sensual or spiritual. Yet, for the most part, we do not find. So we keep on seeking. Arguably, the central desire or motivation in life, over and above the instinct for physical survival, is a desire for

---

[13] *Systematic Collection* Progress in Perfection 6.

wholeness and integration. We experience this as a response to our intuition that things are not quite right, that they could or should be otherwise. And then of course there is the knowledge that one day we will die. Our revolt against mortality seems to spring from the very core of our being, which cannot accept the inherent contradiction that would be non-being. The most obvious manifestation of the will to be is undoubtedly the sex drive, which can be found lurking somewhere in the background of pretty much every desire, impulse, and motivation we have. This too can be reduced to an even more primal generative principle: a profound rejection of the idea of our non-existence. Just as consciousness cannot conceive of nothing, for the simple reason that consciousness implies, by definition, con-sciousness *of something*, so we intuitively feel that that which is – Being itself – cannot *not be*. And the reason we know this is because that, in essence, is what we are.

It is often said that we live in a society in which everyone is 'searching for something'. More specifically, they are searching, we are to infer, for some kind of 'spiritual' fulfilment. Sometimes my naturally sceptical disposition makes me think this is just one of those lazy platitudes we have all taken for granted, like the air we breathe. But it might be true. Even if it would be going too far to suggest that everyone is consciously searching for spiritual fulfilment, I do believe everyone is seeking fulfilment, and that this – by defini-tion – is a spiritual concern, even when only expressed as an instinctive feeling that there must be 'something more' to life than this. Thus, if by spirituality we mean such reflections on the experi-ence of being human as are concerned with what really matters – the meaning and purpose of our lives – then I have to admit it is certainly true for me. So yes, I recognize in myself the hunger for spirituality, for meaning and fulfilment, that people often talk about. Whether this hunger was placed there by an advertising agency or God I cannot say, but either way it seems I have been searching for as long as I can remember.

Following that first defining moment of insight into the Buddhist truth of impermanence and suffering, I started to read avidly – philosophy, literature, psychology, mysticism – in search of a deeper understanding of life. Although I had rejected Christianity, I was somehow attracted to Eastern religions, perhaps because – like many people in modern western societies who find themselves unconvinced by the merits of Christianity – it seemed that Buddhism offered some of the positive aspects of religion without the bits that are impossible to believe. But reading is an essentially private enterprise. Consequently my engagement with spiritual matters was entirely conditioned by the modern assumption that religion belongs to a realm of purely personal experience. Eventually, however, I reached a point in my life where just reading about it was not enough. I had to learn how to do it.

I was twenty-seven, and living – in somewhat primitive conditions – on a small sailing boat on the Isle of Wight. I had been drinking heavily for about ten years and my life was going nowhere fast. Looking back I can see that I was profoundly miserable, though I was not fully aware of it at the time. After leaving school I had just drifted aimlessly, living in different parts of the country, always moving on after a year or so. I worked intermittently – usually as a porter, cleaner or handyman – but could not hold down a job for more than a few months, and inevitably got fired from a few of them because of my drinking. At the same time I was trying to follow my dream of being an artist. Or a writer. Or a musician. Or whatever. But because the dreams I chased remained beyond my grasp, I drank ever more heavily to avoid facing my demons of frustration and despair.

There were, no doubt, a whole host of text-book psychological reasons for all this, but in simple terms I think I was just disappointed – as many of us are – that life was not living up to my expectations. It probably didn't help that I also had a strong self-destructive streak, and lacked confidence. Slowly it began to dawn on me that I was drinking myself into oblivion, perhaps even deliberately. Like the prodigal son, I was throwing away my inheritance – both metaphorically and literally. More or less permanently drunk, by the time I hit rock-bottom I had essentially given up on life. Eventually, the wake-up call came when a close friend drowned somewhere between leaving the pub and going back to his boat. That, a few drunken accidents of my own, and the inexorable disintegration of a long-term relationship, finally made it clear that all was not quite as it should be. The combination of my growing desire to learn more about meditation, and the realization that I needed to get my head together, sort my life out, and address the problem of my drinking forced me to do something decisive. I gave away everything I owned – books, paintings, and a much cherished record collection – and went to India, like so many before and since, in search of enlightenment. I had my last drink on the plane.

As it happens it was the beginning of Lent, though I don't suppose I was aware of that at the time. I visited Bodhgaya, site of the Buddha's enlightenment, and sat under the famous Bodhi tree.

I watched as pilgrims came to pray at the shrine, do their prostrations, or just playfully try to catch the falling leaves for good luck. After a few days spent listening to the mournful drone of Tibetan trumpets, and fending off the 'assistance' of entrepreneurial children offering guided tours, I headed to Varanasi, checked into a guesthouse on the Ghats, and started to look for a guru. A sign in a narrow back street advertised meditation classes, so I signed up.

On a little raised dais at one end of a dimly lit room sat a rather plump middle-aged Indian man. There were half a dozen westerners. He told us to touch our toes, stand on our heads, and sit cross-legged. I couldn't help but notice that he did not actually demonstrate any of these exercises himself. I don't think he could have even if he had wanted to. At the end of the session we all reverently deposited fifty rupees at his feet and solemnly departed. To be honest I found the whole thing rather odd, but still, I had come a long way for this, so I went back for more the following day. At the end of the second class I complained that I wanted to learn how to meditate, not to do a shoulder-stand. He said that I needed to discipline the body in order to train the mind. After giving it some thought I had to agree that he might have a point, even if he did not seem to be a particularly good example of his own philosophy. As many people will know from all too painful experience, it is hard to sit still for any length of time: our bodies are just not used to it. After a couple of weeks in Kathmandu – where I found a rather more dynamic teacher – I went to Rishikesh, checked into an ashram, and applied myself to the training in earnest.

Once I had taken the rather drastic step of leaving the UK, giving up alcohol was surprisingly easy. It took a lot longer, however, for my

body to regain some sort of physiological equilibrium. A few months after I stopped drinking I noticed that I was constantly craving sweet things – cake, chocolate, ice-cream, biscuits, pastries, doughnuts – anything, as long as it contained sugar. To begin with I thought this was simply a consequence of my monastic lifestyle, a reaction against being unable to eat whatever I wanted. Later I learned that it is quite common, when people give up alcohol, for the body to compensate by demanding sugar. At times I would be so obsessed by these cravings that I could think of little else; even when supposedly meditating I would actually be fantasizing about chocolate cake. Sometimes my desperation would become so unbearable that I would guiltily sneak off on some spurious pretext to gorge myself on sweets and chocolate in a vain attempt to appease the yearning. What really amazed me, however, was quite how much chocolate I was capable of eating without feeling sick, or indeed satisfied. It took at least a year to get back to normal.

Other than that, the whole process was relatively straightforward. Cutting myself off from all my old friends and familiar haunts undoubtedly helped – as did the fact that India is not a drinking culture – but more importantly I had better things to do with myself than just getting wasted all the time. I had, very simply, flicked a mental switch, changing my attitude to life from negative and self-destructive to positive and engaged. I no longer *wanted* to drink because I had a new sense of direction and purpose that was more compelling than being drunk: I had a reason to be sober. One spring morning, about six weeks after leaving England, I was sitting on the banks of the river Ganges at Rishikesh. With growing excitement it suddenly dawned on me that I had made a life-changing discovery.

I had found something that felt really worthwhile and fulfilling, something that my life had previously lacked. I decided that I would give up drink, drugs, and all my old ways for good, and – as corny as it may sound – from that moment onwards dedicate myself to the spiritual path, wherever it might lead, and whatever it might involve. It was essentially a conversion experience – death of the old self, and birth of the new – and I was filled with a profound joy, for I knew that I had made the momentous decision to embark upon the only journey that was ever worth making.

If spirituality is about anything, it is surely about transformation, and that transformation is what we are talking about when we talk about conversion. Conversion implies an experience of transcendence, an encounter with something profoundly and mysteriously 'other' than oneself, which forces us out of the realm of the known – our familiar self in other words – and cracks the hard but brittle shell of who we think we are. Having such an experience could hardly be anything but radically life-changing: I had turned my mind towards what really matters, and was seeking a way to be true to who and what I was really meant to be. Shortly after making my decision to take up this new life, I felt an unexpected urge to go to church, just out of curiosity. It was as if my experiences of yoga and meditation, which had brought me into contact with Hindu philosophy, were leading me towards a more mature understanding of God than the one I had rejected as a teenager. Somehow it seemed easier to comprehend such matters when approaching them from a novel perspective. I even began to wonder whether it might be interesting to read the Bible. But after thirteen years of militant atheism, it was hard enough to admit this desire to myself privately, never mind to act upon it publicly.

One day, on the spur of the moment, I took the plunge. It was Easter Sunday 1994. I knew there was a church nearby because I had seen the signs giving directions to it, but I had never noticed the building itself. I soon discovered why. The tiny Christian community in Rishikesh worshipped in what was, as far as I could tell, the pastor's house. I arrived to find the congregation seated in a circle on the floor, around an array of butter lamps burning in the middle of the room. We sang devotional chants, accompanied by a varied assortment of hand-held percussion instruments, cymbals and shakers, played more or less randomly – or so it seemed – by whoever felt inclined to join in. The service was like nothing I had ever experienced before, and since the liturgy was in Hindi (I think), I didn't actually understand a word of it. But as I walked back to the ashram, I had a spring in my step and a huge grin on my face. I felt incredibly happy, as if I had finally come home, like the prodigal son again, after a long exile. Receiving communion for the first time since confirmation felt strangely liberating. I had finally dared to do something that for years I had confidently assumed was stupid and pointless, but which nonetheless now made me feel good. Through my deepening understanding of Indian religion, especially in its devotional forms, I had found a roundabout way back to a religious and cultural identity I could claim as my own, and I distinctly remember feeling a wonderful sense of elation and relief.

In those days I knew nothing about Antony or the desert fathers. I would not have called myself a Christian, and I certainly had no intention of becoming a priest; but I knew I had found the path that I had been looking for – even if I didn't yet know where it would lead me.

CHAPTER THREE

Just Trying to be Normal

*S*unna means 'empty' in Pali – the language of early Buddhism – and if it wasn't for the sign at the top of the drive, one could have been forgiven for thinking that the aptly named 'Sunnataram Forest Monastery' was just an empty field about an hour north of Auckland. The monastery compound was bordered on one side by a neighbouring farm and on the other by a river running through the trees at the bottom of a hill. In it was an old corrugated iron cowshed, open at one end, which served as the main communal living area. Nearby there was a wooden *sala* (an open-sided pavilion), which had been built to house the Buddha image, and use as a prayer hall. The six monks, all from Thailand, lived either in a couple of caravans that were parked around the edge of the field, or else in little wooden huts, called *kutis*, that they were in the process of building in the woods. Rainwater was collected off the roof of the *sala* and stored in large drums for drinking. In winter taking a bath meant a bucket of river water heated in a big cauldron over a wood fire; in summer it was just the river itself. The lavatory was a plywood hut over a hole in the ground.

It was August 1994. I had just arrived in New Zealand from India, and was visiting some relatives who, knowing of my interest in such matters, had taken me to meet the monks. After lunch the Abbot,

Phra Chusit, asked me if I would like to stay a couple of days, just to see what it was like.

I was there for the next six months.

I took to monastic life quickly and easily, with an enthusiasm that was rather unexpected, given how much I had hated boarding school. Much to my surprise, I found the rigour of an ascetic discipline to be as joyful as it was demanding; entering into the life, I felt myself being swept along by a powerful current that transformed the very foundations of my identity and worldview. If ever I had been under the impression that Buddhist monks were sombre and intense, it was soon dispelled by my experience of life at Sunnataram where, it seemed, nothing was ever taken too seriously, and our days were filled with playful laughter. Apart from morning and evening sessions of chanting and meditation in the *sala*, and lunch – which had to be eaten before midday – the timetable was quite loosely structured. But there was always plenty to do: huts needed to be built, and I often found myself assisting the novice, Nan Do – who had to do all the cooking – by chopping vegetables and doing the washing up. A couple of the monks were interested in yoga, so I gave them some lessons, and also helped those that wanted it with their English. My main duty, however, was to be their driver. This gave me a central role in the community, as we were several miles from the nearest town and Buddhist monks are not allowed to drive. For the most part, this involved trips into Auckland to visit Thai families, and would usually include lunch in a Thai restaurant. Since Buddhist monks only eat one meal a day, and preparing food to offer the monks is one of the principal ways in which laypeople earn merit, it was often quite a feast.

As every tourist knows, monks are a familiar sight in Thailand. But this does not necessarily mean that the Thai are unusually pious since it is customary for all Thai men to do a stint as a monk at some point in their lives, and there are all sorts of reasons why people think this is a good idea. I knew a man who, when his business was not doing too well, reasoned that rather than going through the books and cutting costs, he should become a monk for a month, and thus reverse his ailing fortunes by clocking up some good merit on his karmic balance sheet. Needless to say, the company went bust. He didn't last the month in the monastery either.

Of the monks I lived with, most of whom were in their twenties, one explained matter-of-factly that he had taken the robe after the death of his father. At the time, I was unable to see any obvious connection between these two events. Later I learned that this is a fairly standard way of expressing one's filial obligations, undertaken in order to earn merit on behalf of the father who might thereby enjoy a more favourable rebirth next time around. Another had recently left university, after taking a degree in law. The impression I got was that he saw being a monk as beneficial to his personal and professional development. It would look good on his CV, and it was a bit of time out before getting caught up in the rat-race. A third came from a family of farmers and had the ruddy complexion of a man who had spent much of his life working outdoors. I never quite managed to figure out why he had become a monk. It occurred to me, given the privileged status monks enjoy in Thai society, that someone from a poor family, with little or no education, could suddenly find themselves elevated to the highest rank, and have politicians, millionaires and royalty quite literally bowing at their feet – simply by becoming a monk.

One afternoon, shortly after my arrival, I wandered over to the cowshed to join the monks for a cup of tea. I found Phra Chusit nursing a baby goat, feeding it milk from a bottle, and beaming like a proud parent. Feral goats are common in New Zealand, where they are considered to be a menace to farmers, and we had several living on our land. I have no idea how the monks had managed to catch the animal, but from the state of their muddy robes, it had clearly been quite a chase. They decided to call it Pui, and together with the yellow Labrador (whose name I forget), he soon became established as a full member of the monastery. From what I could gather, some of the younger monks were missing home and finding it quite hard to adjust to life in a foreign country; having pets seemed to cheer them up a bit. Perhaps by way of further consolation, the Abbot suggested we might like to start a kitchen garden. Strictly speaking, Buddhist monks are required to live entirely off alms given by the laity. This means no farming, no growing of fruit and vegetables; indeed no economically productive work of any description. They have to be completely dependent. But discipline at Sunnataram New Zealand was a little more relaxed – in a number of ways – than it might have been back home, and most of the monks seemed quite okay with that. Over the next few days members of the local Thai community started bringing plants to the monastery. The novice and I were instructed to dig holes, and half-a-dozen young fruit trees were duly planted.

Pui the goat must have thought the gardening project was a splendid idea, as he discovered that the tender young leaves of our new apple trees were much tastier than the tough old grass that grew in the field. We surrounded the plot with fencing. Being a goat, he jumped over it. The monks were slowly beginning to realize that their cute little baby was fast growing up to become an obnoxious adolescent. In short, having a goat around the place was not actually such a great idea after all. They tried tethering him, but he made such an unbearable fuss that rather than put up with his bleating it was preferable to let him roam freely – and suffer the consequences. Having been taken from his mother and raised as a pet – albeit not quite house-trained – he had grown accustomed to being treated as one of the family, and it was too late to do anything to change that. Imitating the dog, he followed Phra Chusit around wherever he went.

During the six months I spent with the monks in New Zealand, I felt happy and free for the first time since early childhood. Slipping effortlessly into the simple, steady rhythm of monastic life, I realized I had discovered something really worthwhile and fulfilling. At last I felt like I was being true to myself, and doing what I was really meant to be doing. I intuitively understood that the whole of creation was in a state of balanced equilibrium: what is simply is. I saw the unity of all being, that in essence I and the universe were one. I was a wave in the ocean, and therefore I was the ocean too. In this euphoric state, all the concerns of everyday life that had once seemed so important just paled into insignificance. I had no interest in money or possessions; my highest aspiration was just to do what I was doing. I didn't even think about sex. Or at least, on the rare occasions that I did, it was with a wry smile at the sheer ridiculousness of the whole silly business. Of course, a spiritual high, like any other, cannot last forever, but while it did, it was pretty damned good. For a few blissful months I walked barefoot in the cool green forest. I was part of the one conscious ocean of being that is life itself. A tree dies here, a seed sprouts there. What is simply is, and I am that.

Every morning I would ask Phra Chusit if we had any appointments that day; whether, in other words, he would need me to drive them into town, or whether I would have the time to myself to read or study. Sometimes, having been told that there were no plans to go out that day, I would just be settling down with a book, or perhaps already meditating, when all of a sudden I would hear the furious honking of a car horn. Emerging from my caravan I would find all the monks robed up and sitting in the back of the minibus: engine running, driver's door open.

"Come on, come on, hurry up! We've got to go now!" The Abbot would shout impatiently.

"But I thought you said . . ."

"Never mind, never mind. Come on, let's go!"

"So, where are we going then?" I would try and say as nonchalantly as possible, even though I would actually be quite irritated that he hadn't told me the plan when I had asked earlier.

"Don't worry," he would reply dismissively, "I'll give you directions. Just drive!" He was always like that, and I am sure he did it on purpose. Although it could be very annoying at the time, it forced me to be in the moment and prevented me from indulging in my own private world where everything was just the way I wanted it to be. Alternatively, he was just winding me up.

One day, however, we got lost.

"So which way do we go now?" I asked with an air of smug satisfaction. But he still wouldn't tell me, preferring instead to carry on issuing directions until we eventually found our destination – by luck, I would like to think, as much as anything else.

Before becoming a monk Phra Chusit had lived in the United States for several years where, among other things, he had worked as a barman at the Whiskey-a-Go-Go, the famous Los Angeles night-club on Sunset Boulevard. Consequently, he not only spoke perfect English, but also had a somewhat incongruous penchant for junk food and Coca-Cola. Since becoming a monk, he had also spent a couple of years studying Zen Buddhism in Korea, and would often encourage me to practise my meditation in a more Zen-like manner. To this end, he gave me a *koan* to meditate on, saying that the practice of concentrating on the breath was all well and good, but that when thoughts arose, as they inevitably do – however well-developed one's powers of concentration – I should simply let them go. As he spoke, I looked towards the river and noticed some leaves bobbing downstream on the current. Just let go . . .

After lunch one day Phra Chusit came up to me as we were washing our bowls and said:

"What colour is the sky?" I looked up. It was a brilliant azure blue, but I said nothing and just smiled at him. Everything we say about the world is also a construction of the world.

"Exactly!" he said, "You got it!" And then he added, "Do you know what this is all about, what we're trying to do here?"

"What?" I replied.

"Just trying to be normal. We're just trying to be normal. You understand?" I did, and it has stayed with me ever since. In a world gone mad, in which everyday life becomes increasingly dysfunctional and alienating, those who follow a spiritual path – far from opting out – are *just trying to be normal*. To live life according to what really matters is to live a stable, integrated life united by a story that makes sense of things; as opposed to a fragmented life of disparate goals and agendas. This is what is so fascinating and indeed beautiful about the religious life: its singularity of focus, the way everything points towards . . . well, God I suppose. Or Reality, or Truth, if you prefer those words. By contrast, what we have come to regard as 'normal' is, when looked at more closely, a life with no unity of purpose, no coherent ethos, no over-arching story, no big picture.

Yet there is something of a paradox here. By the so-called 'normal' standards of the world we live in, monasticism seems, on the face of it, to be rather odd – anything but normal. At the very least, I suspect most of us probably think there is something unusual or abnormal about the self-denial of monastic discipline, possibly because it strikes at the very heart of what we hold dearest: self-determination and sensual pleasure. There is some truth in this. The monastic life is completely unnatural, and many monks and nuns I know are only too well aware of this. In fact, that is the whole point. Monasticism is not 'normal' because it involves a deliberate attempt to put God first. It is deliberately abnormal. But then, when it comes to human beings, the question of what is normal or natural is rather unclear, even at the best of times. Is it 'natural' to fly in an airplane? Or to wear clothes for that matter? Is it 'normal' to spend all day in front of a computer screen? What we call normal life is actually, if we think about it, far from normal. The first Christian monks and nuns renounced the world and everything considered 'normal', withdrawing to the Egyptian desert in order to devote themselves entirely to seeking God. Were they completely mad, or truly sane? Whichever way you look at it, there is clearly something different about monasticism. The priority given to communal rather than personal interests, together with the core principles of silence and humility, make for an ethos that is far from fashionable in today's individualistic consumer culture. What I believe the monastic life shows us, therefore, is what being normal should really look like. To try to be normal in this sense is to stop living through the fantasies and projections that we imagine to be normal: it is to wake up from the daydream, and be ourselves instead.

Now that the notion of 'alternative' has become just another norm, it is the religious life that is truly alternative, for it holds a mirror to society and challenges our commonplace assumptions about what we mean by 'normal' in the first place. In his correspondence with the church at Corinth, Paul wrote that the truth that is God makes worldly wisdom seem foolish. By implication, therefore, God's way must seem like foolishness to the world.[14] These days, many people certainly think that the very idea of monasticism is completely crazy. However, anyone who actually experiences something of the life, and manages to see beyond the stereotypes and clichés, will soon discover that monks and nuns are not only very normal indeed, but often far more well-adjusted than the rest of us. The obvious question is, why should this be so?

One of the things that has struck me most forcefully, as a result of my own encounters with monasticism, is that it is a life lived as a unified whole, focused on that which is of supreme value (whatever 'that' might be). It represents, therefore, an attempt to realize the

---

[14] 1 Corinthians 1.20, 2.14, 3.19.

unity implied by the word 'monk' – derived from the Greek *monos*, literally meaning alone or solitary – which suggests that the monk is one who lives alone with God. This unity can be understood in various different ways. The monk seeks unity with God, and with the truth of who they are. The monk's life is one in which all the component parts are united by a single focus: Antony was described as having achieved 'singleness of heart'. This 'one-pointedness' is what makes the monastic life the exact opposite of our so-called 'normal' lives, which tend to be highly fragmented and compartmentalized, to the extent that we even talk about our home life, our family life, our work life, our social life, our spiritual life and so on – as if they were all separate.

For all its peculiarities and contradictions, the religious life is at heart a way of being in the world that is completely unified, whose every aspect is turned wholly towards God. To be a monk or nun is to be pointed towards what really matters, motivated by values that ultimately promise a greater freedom than that to be gained by simply indulging every whim and fancy. With its insistence that the individual can only be properly formed in community, which often means subordinating self to other – whether that other is conceived as God or as neighbour – monasticism represents a radical alternative to the unfettered egotism and subsequent alienation that seems so characteristic of contemporary society. Indeed, the monastic life is as radically counter-cultural today as it ever was, for it demands the complete inversion of everything we take for granted, requiring us – in the words of the Gospel – to lose our life in order to find it.

In spite of my long-standing interest in Buddhism, I had not been staying in the monastery for long when I began to realize that my grasp of its teachings was very superficial indeed. I knew that Buddhists did not believe in any such thing as an immortal soul. To be more exact, they maintain that if you analyse the experience of selfhood, you will find no permanent unchanging entity that can be considered to be a self, as such, but only a series of impersonal processes that are neither stable nor essential. What we call the self amounts, therefore, to a case of mistaken identity. Wishing to clarify matters, I asked Phra Chusit how, if there is no self in Buddhism, there can be rebirth. In other words, who or what is reborn? Or, for that matter, attains Nirvana? Phra Chusit sighed wearily. As I have since discovered on numerous occasions, it is the one question everyone always asks.

"You have to understand this doctrine of *anatta*, or 'not-self', properly. You can't just figure it out in your head; you have to see it for yourself. Then you will realize this question is meaningless." Undeterred, I asked Phra Chusit if he thought reincarnation was really true. He said that was the wrong question too, but – in what struck me as a Buddhist version of Pascal's wager – he said that it was good to believe it, and to live life *as if* it were true, for doing so would make one a better person. I took his point. After all, to acknowledge our part in a story that continues beyond us is to acknowledge our responsibility for the future consequences of our present actions; it is to make ourselves accountable to something other than our immediate personal preferences. But surely such a story had to be more than just a useful fiction? Surely it needed to be really true as well, in order for it to be truly compelling? I mean, if none of it is *really* true then why bother? If it is all ultimately nonsense, if life really is meaningless and pointless, then are we not wasting our time with religion, when we could at least be going out and having a good time? Peering cautiously into the void, I caught a glimpse of the dangerous truth lurking behind all the stories we tell ourselves.

Six months later the fruit trees were almost dead and all attempts at starting a vegetable garden had long been abandoned. Pui the goat had become an uncontrollable nuisance. The monks decided to try and lose him, so one afternoon we went for a long walk in the woods. Pui was left bleating on the other side of a gate while we ran off into the trees, but he found his way back to the compound before nightfall. On another occasion, I was distracted from my reading by the sound of excited barking. I looked up to see two monks in a canoe, the goat in the middle, the dog swimming behind them. Some hours later, the monks returned. They had paddled as far upstream as they could go, deposited the goat on the bank, and paddled back again. This time they thought they'd cracked it. I pointed out that wherever they had left the goat, it was probably on land that belonged to a farmer – we were surrounded by market gardeners – and that any farmer who found a stray goat on their land would shoot it without a second thought. The monks looked concerned. Three days later, a rather bedraggled-looking Pui returned home, wagging his tail.

Pui became something of a barometer of the community's morale, and all the signs indicated that things were not going too well. The Abbot was often away, and two of the other monks had gone to Australia. In the meantime, a visiting French monk called Ajahn Thitanano had arrived, wanting to enjoy some time in the peace and tranquillity of our forest retreat. Relatively rare among western converts for having stuck at it, he had been in robes for more than twenty years, spoke fluent Thai, and was respected by the Thai community as a venerable teacher. In Phra Chusit's absence, he became the most senior monk at Sunnataram.

One day, I was summoned to the cowshed. A noisy discussion was taking place between the assembled monks and a group of laypeople who had dropped by for the afternoon. Ajahn Thitanano beckoned me over. He had a road atlas open in front of him.

"Right, what you need to do is take the goat in the minibus and drive out to this area here." He pointed to the map. "It's at least a hundred miles away. Put the goat out and come back."

"What! Are you serious?" I was astounded. Forgetting all the rules of etiquette – of which there are many when it comes to dealing with monks – I took a deep breath and said:

"No, I can't do that. It's a nature reserve." There was a strained silence. The Thai treat their monks with the utmost deference: my forthright disobedience was almost unthinkable to them, and I was all too aware of their disapproving glances.

"Exactly! That's why we chose it," continued Ajahn Thitanano breezily. "The goat will be safe there, it's a good place for him."

"No, you don't understand. It's a nature reserve. It's protected. It's protected against things like goats. A goat is a pest in this country." There was an animated exchange in Thai.

"I see . . . Right. Well, maybe here then." He jabbed his finger at another area of the map, a bit further up the coast.

"No." I said bluntly. The Thai lay-people started muttering among themselves, clearly outraged by my total lack of respect towards a monk. "You just can't do this," I continued, with a tremor in my voice. "I'm not taking that goat anywhere. You can't just abandon it after taking it away from its mother and raising it as a pet. You can't just throw it out because you don't like having it around any more." I stormed out, on the verge of tears, and more than a little alarmed at the vehemence of my own anger.

Like I said, all was not well at Sunnataram. When Phra Chusit returned I told him that I had decided to go back to India. Not because of the business with the goat, but because I was getting restless anyway. He was disappointed, and I was sorry to be leaving, but the time had come and I had to move on.

CHAPTER FOUR
What Really Matters

March 21, 1995. Rishikesh. 4 am. The moment I was conscious of being conscious, I opened my eyes, sat up, and knelt on the bed. After a year without a clock, I was getting quite adept at the trick of waking up when I wanted to. Racing against the legion of thoughts rushing to crowd in on my mind, I offered a quick prayer to Saraswati, Hindu goddess of wisdom, before swinging my feet to the ground. Other than Swami Brahmananda, whom I would usually pass on my way to the wash-room, the rest of the ashram was still sound asleep. It would be at least an hour before the first glow of dawn would be greeted by the spluttering sound-system of the temple opposite.

I lit a candle and an incense stick, filling the room with the sweet aroma of sandalwood, wrapped myself in a rough woollen shawl, and sat cross-legged on the floor. I breathed in and I breathed out, repeating a simple phrase, while trying not to get caught up in the thoughts that came and went as they pleased, largely unthought. Two hours later I stretched out my legs – numb with pain by now – and stood to perform twelve salutations to the sun, quietly intoning the appropriate mantras as I worked my way through the cycle. Then a series of yoga postures and breathing exercises – another two hours – before getting dressed and strolling into the village. It was barely nine o'clock. Shopkeepers were raising their shutters, restaurant owners offering the first fruits of their clay ovens – maybe a chapatti or two – to the passing cows. I bought some provisions and went back to the ashram to eat my only meal of the day: a large bowl of fruit and yoghurt followed by a few biscuits. On the eleventh day of each half of the lunar month, the traditional Hindu day of abstinence, I would skip this meal altogether to do a forty-eight hour fast. I once asked a swami why it was the eleventh day, as opposed to any other, but he didn't seem to know.

I spent the hours from about ten o'clock until four in the afternoon studying Hindu and Buddhist scriptures, commentaries, and textbooks. I learnt about Vedic astrology and Ayurvedic medicine, and started to teach myself Sanskrit. I also read the Bible and the Qu'ran. By four o'clock it was time to do another two hours of fairly vigorous yoga. In the evening I allowed myself a couple of hours to relax. I took a bath – meaning a bucket of cold water – and sat on the balcony outside my room to enjoy the golden hour as the sun gently sank behind the temples lining the far side of the river. At eight o'clock I lit a candle, wrapped myself in my rough woollen shawl again and sat cross-legged on the floor, breathing in and breathing out. Two hours later I went to bed.

It was an absurdly strict regime, physically and mentally. But fired up with the greedy zeal of the newly converted, I became spiritually drunk, imagining that I was somehow in deep communion with the rhythms of the cosmos, that I could feel the phases of the moon and read the underlying patterns and hidden motivations in people's behaviour. I don't know how long I managed to keep it going. Several months, at least. Until eventually, nearing the brink of exhaustion and perhaps the limits of my sanity, I realized I needed to come back down to earth. Gradually I relaxed my discipline, which was in any case entirely self-imposed, and tentatively re-established contact with the rest of the human race.

One of the first people I met was Walter, an American who had been living in Rishikesh for over twenty years. He knew all the gurus. And the charlatans. But unlike most people out there, he could tell the difference. The most remarkable thing about Walter, however, is that to this day he is the only person I have ever known who has told me unbelievable things that I could find no reason to disbelieve. I mean, he wasn't like those people who are always talking about astral projection, past lives, and ascended masters. Nor was he obviously crazy like the guy who knocked on my door one evening complaining about the 'rays' that the Vatican, CIA, and assorted others were apparently using to control his mind. You can spot those ones immediately, just by the look in their eyes. No, Walter was different. Very down to earth, he had nothing to prove, and no discernible reason to lie. I still don't know what to make of the stories he told me. In any case, through him I started to attend the daily *darshan*, or audience with the guru, in one of the neighbouring ashrams.

When I knew Swami Krishnananda he was already quite elderly and frail, and living in a set of rooms on the top floor of the ashram's small charitable hospital. Every morning he would come out of his room and sit in a chair in the hallway, which would be full of people sitting on the floor waiting to see him. The ensuing hour could consist of anything from mundane ashram business to advanced spiritual instruction. Often foreigners would come asking for initiation, which he would always refuse, telling them there was nothing to gain from collecting spiritual souvenirs. That's what I liked about him: no bullshit. He had a formidable reputation, both as a scholar and as a guru, and people of all sorts – from government ministers to illiterate villagers – would come from far and wide to sit at his feet. Indeed, his authority inspired such awe and reverence that I found him very intimidating. Every afternoon, the same thing would happen except that instead of a discussion there would be an hour of silent meditation. Despite all the noise of a busy Indian road, clearly audible through the open windows – not to mention the cries of children receiving their vaccinations in the out-patient clinic downstairs – the silence that surrounded him was absolute. It was as if his charisma held everyone's mind in perfect stillness.

I had been attending these twice-daily meetings for some months when one morning at *darshan* Krishnananda suddenly turned to me and said:

"Who are you? What are you doing here? You come and sit here every day, but you never say anything!"

I was utterly petrified.

"I'm coming just to be here. . ." I replied nervously.

"Yes, but *what* are you doing here? Are you practising some meditations?"

"Yes, I am."

"How are you meditating?" he barked. So I told him that I meditated by quietly observing and letting go of the thoughts as they arose, trying at the same time not to get personally involved in the activity of the mind.

"Yes, yes, that's okay," he said, chopping and slicing the air between us with his hands. "At least, to begin with. But eventually there comes a point when you have to affirm something. Even after you deny everything, there is still something left, some pure awareness. You have to say yes to that."

Swami Krishnananda often used to explain that the self could not be identical to the body, because if I were to – let us say – lose a leg, I would still think of myself as a whole person, I would still be *me*. Therefore, he maintained, the self must be a centre of consciousness somehow separate from the physical body. The same argument can be applied to the mind. I cannot be my memories, for example, because if I forget something, I am not fundamentally diminished as a result. I am still me. In fact, whatever it is that is me cannot be identified with anything mental or physical that is subject to change, because then I would not be the same person now that I was at some point in the past, such as when I was a child. And yet I am still me. For all these reasons, therefore, the 'true' self – whatever that might mean – must be located elsewhere, beyond the self of ordinary experience. He encouraged us to imagine ourselves as a centre of consciousness, animating and extending throughout the entire universe.

"So why not do it the other way? Say yes to everything. Instead of saying 'not this, not this', how about if you say 'I am'. Imagine your consciousness expanding beyond your body to include all the objects in the room: the table in front of you, the chair, the room itself, the mountains outside, the sun and the moon, the whole solar system and the galaxy, until you become one with the universal cosmic consciousness!"

I nodded enthusiastically, hoping the interrogation would soon be over.

"But it's very difficult, very difficult . . ." he muttered, before moving on to the next person. The exchange left me feeling vulnerable and self-conscious, but afterwards Walter said how lucky I had been to have had the attention.

Although he was by then retired, Walter had previously worked for many years as a senior instructor in one of the principal yoga centres. He told me how easy it was to spot the people who did yoga by the way they strutted about like peacocks. I suspect he was gently trying to tell me something. As I learned more about yoga I discovered that the original Indian texts do not place as much emphasis as one might expect on the physical exercises and postures that we typically associate with yoga in the west. Indeed, they appear to be more concerned with purification rituals primarily intended, it would seem, to divert the sexual energies of teenage boys. This is not to say that yoga is not a good and useful thing to do, but that it is at most a complement to a spiritual practice, rather than an intrinsically spiritual discipline in itself; especially when divorced from the complex religious philosophy of which it is but a small part, and without which it is, literally, just a posture. Nevertheless, due to the popularity of a number of modern teachers, it is the 'gymnastics' that people most commonly tend to equate with yoga. This is all the more confusing because properly speaking the word yoga is a generic term that *does* in fact refer to spiritual practice, especially prayer and meditation.

But why even do that? I mean, why meditate? Why have anything to do with religion or spirituality in the first place? We need to be able to answer this question because presumably there would not be any need for it at all unless we thought there was something wrong, a problem requiring a solution. The need for religion or a spiritual practice rests on the assumption that things – the world, life in general, myself – are, or are experienced as being, somewhat less than perfect. In addition to the obvious manifestations of physical suffering – violence, sickness, poverty – there is also what we might call existential suffering, variously expressed in notions such as the Judeo-Christian allegory of the Fall, and the Buddhist doctrine of *duhkha*. Like Tantalus, the character in Greek mythology punished by being confined to a pool whose waters he could not drink and overhung by grapes he could not reach, we experience this as the frustration of not getting what we want, being driven to pursue desires that cannot be fulfilled, and the disappointment of never being satisfied. This is what we might call the problem, whether real or imagined, of being human. Waking up to it presents us with the fundamental motivation for spiritual practice.

Perhaps some people will say they are perfectly content as they are and with what they have got. If so, then they are very fortunate indeed. I know I would not be able to make that claim myself because there are so many things I want to do, and that I would like to change about the circumstances of my life. Indeed, just a little self-examination reveals that I am constantly imagining things being other than as they are. As I started to learn a bit about how the mind works, I became increasingly aware of this discrepancy between who I am and who I want to be. I very much doubt I am any different from anyone else in this respect: one way or another, we are all trying to be or become something other than who and what we are at present.

So everything is not all right as it is, otherwise we would not be constantly seeking satisfaction; whether of our physical desires, professional ambitions, or personal goals. Even if we are consciously aware that the pursuit of all the things we think we want will not bring us lasting contentment, we are still driven – in everything we do – by a subconscious impulse to attain whatever it is we imagine would constitute perfect fulfilment. All our desires, including those directed towards sensual pleasures and worldly achievements, conceal this more profound and, by definition, spiritual yearning for ultimate peace and contentment. In a sense, therefore, the desire for God and the desire for the world are essentially the same, though differently oriented: even the most incorrigible pleasure-seeker is really seeking God, or that which is the point of everything. But the hedonist needs to ask themselves whether the 'god' they worship is really worthy of the name, whether the pursuit of pleasure actually delivers the satisfaction they seek. I suspect not, otherwise rich people would be content with what they have got, and powerful people would be at peace with the world, whereas more often than not the exact opposite is the case.

Most spiritual traditions teach that our desires must be disciplined. This tends to give people the impression that the life of renunciation requires desire to be entirely suppressed. Desire is natural, we complain. Quite so, but that is not the point. Nobody is suggesting that desire is 'wrong' as such; rather that simply indulging our every whim will not result in the fulfilment we seek. It is not that enjoyment should not be enjoyed, but that chasing after enjoyment for its own sake inevitably ceases to be enjoyable. Desire is of course natural, good, and apart from anything else, a fundamental necessity; arguably the essential characteristic of Being itself. At its most basic, desire is an expression of the irreducible fact of existence: the will to be that is what is. Desire is therefore a necessary part of what it is to be human, and we cannot ignore that. St Antony said that we should expect to be tempted until our last breath, and echoing him down the ages, a monk I know is fond of saying that our desires will not cease until the last nail is banged into our coffin. This does not mean desire must be suppressed, but that its objects need to be chosen more thoughtfully. Discipline is thus not about the repression of desire but its redirection.

Desire – or more precisely 'thirst' – was identified by the Buddha as the cause of *duhkha*, the insidious unsatisfactoriness that pervades the whole of life. Interestingly, *duhkha* arises not only because the things we crave – being themselves impermanent – cannot provide lasting satisfaction, but also more subtly because the very notion of the one who desires is based on a misidentification of the sense of self with the phenomena of experience, especially desire and its objects. Thus it is not so much the objects of desire that we need to renounce, but the very idea of being a desiring subject; non-attachment is not so much about giving up our possessions, as giving up the notion of the one who possesses. In other words, first we have to see how who we are is what we want; then that the desires we commonly express are but a cipher masking what we really want, and thus who we really are. This is easier said than done. Motivations are complex: the truly disinterested action – with no personal expectations concerning the outcome – is exceptionally rare. Even seemingly altruistic behaviour is often driven by subtle forms of selfishness. So the question we need to ask is this: 'What do I really, really want, finally?'

Deciding this means working out the difference between what we really want and what we think we want, and that in turn is a question of working out why we are doing what we are doing, and what we hope to achieve by it. Whatever it is that we think we want, it is a projection of what we imagine is required to bring us contentment. Desire is a state of agitation; it is restlessness and frustration. Gratification of desire is a state of quiescence. We may find that what we really want is not the ostensible object of desire, but relief from the agitation that desire causes. Desire is the will to be, but ironically what it really wants is not to be. On this view, the most fundamental desire is actually a desire for the absence of desire. So we have to ask ourselves, 'What *really* matters?' Will the attainment of it bring happiness, peace and satisfaction – completely, absolutely, finally? If we explore this question, what do we get? Ice cream? Yes, ice cream is certainly good, but it is by no means the ultimate. What about sex? Well, sex is important – arguably the basic instinct underlying almost everything we do – but somehow I feel that this still is not it. Ultimate fulfilment has yet to be reached. If we continue this process, we eventually end up with . . . with what? We cannot say. It is just 'what really matters'. This is what people are talking about when they talk about God, the ultimate object of desire.

That we have desire also indicates that we are beings with the capacity for love. Love is absolute, either yes or no; not maybe, not relative, not something that can be measured on a scale of one to ten. Moreover, because it is absolute, it is limitless, infinite, total. Therefore our yearning for fulfilment, our yearning to make this infinite love real and present, can never be satisfied by anything transient, finite, or limited; can never be satisfied by anything less than an object that is itself limitless, infinite and total. The limited satisfaction of attaining a finite object of desire can only be temporary. Like the object itself, it will pass and our thirst will remain unquenched. Instead of satisfaction we will feel only emptiness;

rather than contentment we will experience lack. It is as if there is an empty hole inside us, which we are desperately trying to fill – with talk, noise, activity, achievements, experiences and possessions – but, like a black hole in space, it swallows everything: it is insatiable. Logic dictates that if this thirst is infinite, then only the infinite will ever be able to quench it: infinite love will only ultimately find fulfilment in an object that it can love limitlessly and which must therefore itself be infinite. Some would say this inner emptiness reveals our yearning for God.

At the same time there is also a sense in which love cannot be satisfied – as such – by an infinite and limitless object, for the infinite love of an infinite object will never reach an end or pass away, but rather grow and grow infinitely. The true fullness of perfect satisfaction, which can only be realized in an infinite love for the infinite, only becomes possible by giving one's self away, abandoning oneself to this boundless, inexhaustible love that some people call God, the will to be that is what is. Monks I know have spoken of their vocation as similar to being in love. If it is our nature to love, then – according to its practitioners – the monastic life represents a love that forsakes all others: the irresistible, all-consuming love of love itself. In the tradition of the desert fathers this is – paradoxically – declared to be a love that is at the same time born of detachment.

The epigrammatic sayings of the desert fathers present us with the fruit of their practice, but do not in themselves tell us much about the theory underlying it. However, both the theory and practice of desert monasticism are comprehensively – if at times enigmatically – articulated in the writings of Evagrius of Pontus (c. 345–399), arguably the principal systematiser of early monastic theology. Evagrius was, by all accounts, a gifted scholar whose talents were recognized at an early age by Basil of Caesarea. After Basil's death in 379 he served as a deacon under Gregory of Nazianzus in Constantinople during the early 380s, where he became embroiled in a scandalous affair with an aristocratic woman who – inconveniently – also happened to be married. Following a rather alarming dream about being imprisoned and tortured on the orders of the woman's husband, he fled the city and took a ship to Jerusalem, resolving to amend his life. Here he stayed with Rufinus and Melania, the wealthy Roman widow who had founded a monastery on the Mount of Olives. It evidently was not long, however, before he forgot all his good intentions and reverted to his old ways once again – until a serious illness laid him low for six months. In response to Melania's astute diagnosis of the psychic causes of his symptoms, he gave her his word that he would become a monk if and when he recovered. In 383, Evagrius kept his promise and travelled to Egypt, where he became a disciple of both Macarius the Great and Macarius the Alexandrian. In due course he established himself as a highly respected teacher in his own right.

From his writings it is clear that Evagrius was strongly influenced by the brilliant but controversial Origen (c. 185–254), who believed that the goal of human existence is to acquire knowledge (*gnosis*) of our true nature – and, ultimately, knowledge of the God of whom we are the image. In other words, because we are made 'in the image of God', there is an inherent affinity between the mind and God – the deepest reality of what we are. Therefore the mind, if purified, has the potential to know God. This notion, derived from deep identification with the words of Jesus, specifically 'Blessed are the pure in heart, for they will see God',[15] suggests that we may catch a glimpse of God's reflection in the mirror of our souls, polished in the discipline of ascetic practice. Origen was posthumously condemned in 399 and then again at the council of Constantinople in 553 for some of his more unorthodox theories, such as that concerning the pre-existence of souls. Tainted by association, the works of Evagrius were suppressed and all but disappeared from the historical record, remaining largely unknown until relatively recently. Nevertheless, his treatises on stillness, self-examination and prayer have had an enormous – albeit anonymous – effect on the development of Christian spirituality.[16]

The path of spiritual progress is described by Evagrius in terms of three distinct and necessary stages. First of all, the monk needs to cultivate a foundation of stillness (*hesychia*), which in turn is dependent on his withdrawal (*anachoresis*) from the obligations and demands of everyday life. Having established a solid foundation of stillness by becoming a stranger to worldly concerns, the monk embarks upon the second stage, which Evagrius calls the 'practical life'. This involves careful self-examination under the tutelage of an experienced guide, in order to cultivate *apatheia* – which we might translate as impassability, or non-attachment. This in turn is the necessary foundation for the third and final stage: the contemplation of, and

---

[15] Matthew 5.8.

[16] Extracts from the following works of Evagrius: *Eight Thoughts, Eulogios, Exhortations, Foundations, Maxims, On Prayer, On Thoughts, Praktikos,* and *Reflections* taken from the English translations in Robert Sinkewicz (trans.), *Evagrius of Pontus: The Greek Ascetic Corpus* (Oxford: Oxford University Press, 2003).

ultimately union with, God that Evagrius refers to as the 'gnostical life'. The summit of this practice is 'pure prayer', which he describes as a direct knowledge of the inner truth of things, wherein the mind is voided of itself, like the empty sky or a clear blue sapphire, and attains to what he calls 'the place of God'.[17]

In his writings, Evagrius seems to give most attention to the second stage, the 'practical life' of non-attachment, for it is by cultivating *apatheia* – which in turn is the result of mindfulness – that the soul is brought to *gnosis*. A term borrowed from Stoic philosophy, *apatheia* is described by Evagrius as being 'when the mind has begun to see its own light and remains still before the apparitions occurring during sleep and looks upon objects with serenity'.[18] *Apatheia* is not, however, simply the result of outward restraint, but rather the development of an inner detachment; a distinction of which the desert fathers were well aware. In one story a hermit explains that if lust, greed, or vanity are still alive in the heart then they are not destroyed but merely imprisoned. Unless a monk is able to regard a pile of stones and a pot of gold as having the same value, he cannot claim to be beyond the influence of his passions.[19] Evagrius describes monks who had attained *apatheia* as having achieved a degree of non-attachment so profound that even if a snake were to bite their foot while they were praying it would not distract them. In another story we are told of John the Dwarf, who used to pray standing in a cistern of cold water, sometimes for days on end. He was said to have been so deeply absorbed in communion with God that he remained completely

---

[17] Evagrius, *On Thoughts* 39.
[18] Evagrius, *Praktikos* 64.
[19] *Systematic Collection* Discretion 15.

unmoved when a demon in the form of a dragon coiled itself around him, bit off chunks of his flesh, and vomited them back in his face.[20]

We may think of non-attachment in terms of cold indifference – hardly the stuff of Christian charity – yet Evagrius insists that the detachment of which he speaks results not in self-centredness but the very opposite: love. Love, he maintains, is 'the offspring of impassability'.[21] In other words, if non-attachment is understood as the eradication of self-interest, then it is only when this has been accomplished that we can be genuinely open and available to others. This is why Evagrius defines a monk as 'one who is separated from all and united with all'.[22]

---

[20] Evagrius, *On Prayer* 107.
[21] Evagrius, *Praktikos* 81.
[22] Evagrius, *On Prayer* 124.

CHAPTER FIVE

Eight Thoughts

In the *Historia Monachorum* Evagrius is described as 'a wise and learned man [. . .] skilled in the discernment of thoughts, an ability he had acquired by experience'.[23] The 'discernment of thoughts' lies at the very heart of the Evagrian system, for it is by this means that the monk is to acquire *apatheia*. Indeed, his sophisticated psycho-spiritual taxonomy of the eight thoughts (which would end up being popularized as the well-known 'seven deadly sins' of medieval morality) makes Evagrius one of the most significant figures in the Christian spiritual tradition.

Interestingly, when Evagrius talks about the eight generic thoughts – gluttony, lust, avarice, sadness, anger, acedia, vanity and pride – he seems to refer to them as both 'thoughts' and as 'demons', as if these terms were synonymous. It is hard to know what to make of this. To the modern reader Evagrius may appear to be suggesting a metaphorical understanding of demons consistent with contemporary usage: after all, we often talk about people acting as if they are possessed, and it is not hard to imagine how something like our collective obsession with celebrities might be described similarly. The Greek word in question, *logismoi*, refers to those obsessive thoughts that develop a life of their own, that consume us, and literally occupy or

---

[23] Russell, *Lives*, p. 107.

possess us. But this does not necessarily mean that Evagrius thought demons were merely metaphorical. He clearly writes as if he believed they were real, manifesting themselves to ascetics through their thoughts. Having cut himself off from the world, the monk leaves the demons with no option but to attack on the only front remaining: the mind. To put it another way, when you renounce everything you are left alone with nothing but your thoughts, which can then become all-consuming.

I do not know exactly how real demons were to Evagrius, but I do think it would betray a dreary lack of imagination on our part if we were to assume that demons are 'just' thoughts. Not because this fails to recognize the reality of demons (about which I make no claim to expertise), but because it fails to recognize the reality of thoughts and the very real power of the imagination to shape the world we experience. There is nothing unreal about the tangible effects that obsessive thoughts can sometimes have, which is why – when reading Evagrius – one is immediately struck by the precision of his astute and closely observed understanding of the human mind and its behaviour.

Before examining each of the thoughts in turn, it is worth noting that even the order in which they are listed is significant. Thus, if we succumb to gluttony, lust is likely to be trailing close behind, opening the door to the influence of other desires including avarice. Having one's desires frustrated will inevitably give rise to sadness and anger, followed by the onslaught of apathy; while achieving any degree of success against these thoughts will make us susceptible to vanity and pride. This reflects the logic of spiritual progress: first one must purify the sensual dimension, then the emotional, and finally the intellectual. Note also that they are listed in order of increasing strength: they get progressively more difficult to overcome.

The first and often most troubling of the *logismoi* is gluttony. Scarcity of food, and the basic imperative to survive under extremely harsh conditions, presented one of the most acute problems for the monk living in the desert. Gluttony in this context, therefore, cannot mean the same to the desert fathers – who lived on an impossibly frugal diet of bread and water – as it does to us. According to Palladius, Evagrius was supposed to have subsisted on a pound of bread per day and a pint of oil every three months. He abstained entirely from fresh fruit and vegetables, and only ate cooked food – a little gruel – in the last years of his life when illness dictated it. Clearly, gluttony does not here refer to opulent feasts, exotic delicacies and the finest wines. It is not excess the desert fathers were concerned with, but rather a morbid concern with the health and welfare of the body. This should sound familiar: after all, we live in a society of excessive consumption and profligate waste that is at the same time obsessed with health and fitness, dieting, and image. These are two manifestations of the same problem.

Like all demons, the demon of gluttony is devious, and will use subtle tactics. If a monk has succeeded in practising severe austerities, to the point of damaging his health, gluttony may tempt him to try and distract others. It will persuade the monk to 'visit those who are practising abstinence and to tell them of their misfortunes and how they came about as a result of their asceticism'.[24]

---

[24] Evagrius, *Praktikos* 7.

As I found when I began to practise a spiritual discipline, a troubling preoccupation with food is likely to be among the first of the trials one is likely to face. The desert fathers maintained that controlling the desires of the flesh with regard to eating was the first step towards mastering the unruly conduct of the mind: abstinence, they believed, would keep the mind alert and curb any tendency towards sensuality. Their regime may seem austere to us, but in context it should be seen as balanced. Abba Poemen is recorded as having said, 'I think it better that one should eat every day, but only a little, so as not to be satisfied.'[25] He goes on to describe this balanced discipline as the 'royal way'.

The demon of gluttony cannot be fully comprehended in isolation from the demon of lust, for according to the ancient Greek medical theory of the humours, food was directly linked to sex. Consequently, the desert fathers believed that nothing was more guaranteed to stir up sensual thoughts than the lethargy induced by a full belly. This is why Evagrius describes gluttony as 'the mother of fornication', and warns that the demons will often try and tempt a monk to gluttony first, before bringing him to complete ruin with lust.[26] Hence the desert monastics eschewed the eating of meat: not in order to avoid cruelty to animals, but because meat, being a primary source of the moist humour, was understood to contribute to the production of semen. A dry, salty diet on the other hand, consisting of bread and occasionally olives or lentils would, it was supposed, help to inhibit lustful tendencies: hence Evagrius advises his visitors

---

[25] *Alphabetical Collection* Poemen 31.
[26] Evagrius, *Eight Thoughts* 2.1

not to drink too much water, for the demons 'frequently light on well-watered places'.[27]

It will probably come as no surprise to learn that it was – and no doubt still is – common for monks to be plagued by sexual fantasies by day and erotic dreams by night. As with the demon of gluttony, the demon of lust is cunning, and does not always attack head-on. Instead it may try and persuade the monk that sex is natural – which of course it is – and therefore that abstinence, especially for the young and vigorous, is unnatural, even though in fact this does not necessarily follow. After all, just because it may be healthy to, let us say, drink a glass of wine a day, it does not therefore mean that it is unhealthy not to. Interestingly, Evagrius describes lust as a form of idolatry: the misplaced worship of a false image based on a delusion rather than the true image of a real person. To lust after someone is to see them as an object, a means to the satisfaction of one's selfish ends, and not as a subject and an end in themselves. It is to violate the integrity of a person as a person, and a failure to see others as we see ourselves.

Of course monks are not merely trying to confine their lust within socially acceptable parameters (which anyone might consider reasonable); they practise celibacy, and that is something most of us are not going to be signing up for. Nor am I suggesting we should. Nonetheless, it might be interesting to think about what is going on here. Perhaps because we live in such a highly sexualized culture, we tend to focus on celibacy as the defining feature of monastic life. In some ways it is. Celibacy epitomizes a radical break with social

---

[27] Russell, *Lives*, p. 107.

conventions, and in any case, by definition, monks are single. Yet far from repressing sexuality as if one could pretend it does not exist, the monastic tradition recognizes the reality of sexual desire, but also maintains that it can be expressed in terms of a commitment to an exclusive relationship with God and the love of all creation. In theory at least, celibacy frees monks and nuns from relationships coloured by self-serving agendas: it is not that sex is 'bad' *per se*, but that there are other uses to which that energy can be put. Having said that, I cannot imagine many people these days going quite as far as Evagrius in their attempts to banish unwelcome thoughts: he once spent a whole night standing naked in a well during winter. This may be a little excessive, but it is only an extreme example of a fairly ordinary – and very effective – procedure with which most of us are probably familiar: the substitution of one distraction for another. Moderation in diet, intense prayer, and strenuous manual work were all recommended for that very reason. As one desert hermit puts it: 'Ever since I became a monk, I have never taken my fill of bread, or water, or sleep, and because I am tormented by desire for food, I cannot feel the pricks of lust.'[28]

Christian asceticism has often been criticized for denying the body, especially in terms of our sexuality. Contrary to what may be supposed, however, sexual abstinence was not in fact a Christian innovation. In pagan Roman culture, sex was considered to be debilitating; virility consisted in preserving one's 'vital spirit', thus making continence an indication of strength. The Christians did, however, take things further, viewing the renunciation of sex as a means of

---

[28] *Systematic Collection* Lust 31.

rising above our animal instincts towards the divine. Celibacy also came to be seen as a sort of metaphorical martyrdom, and therefore a fast-track to heaven. The connection between sex and death can be made in other ways too: from the notion of procreation as a sub-conscious attempt to overcome death, it is but a short step to the view that sex is in fact the cause of death. In other words, sex brings life into being, but life ends in death. So by renouncing sex some ascetics believed they were cheating death of further prey, thereby undoing the consequences of the Fall and hastening their return to union with God. I am not suggesting for one moment that everyone has to be celibate in order to be spiritual: the point is we need to understand the relationship between inner and outer discipline. While monastic asceticism seems to be primarily focused on control of the body, this is to be seen as intimately linked with control of the mind, and *vice versa*. Being a monk involves the whole person: a unity of body, mind and spirit.

As with gluttony and lust, the demon of avarice also preys on anxieties concerning the body, specifically with regard to the wealth and property needed to ensure our physical comfort, both now and in the future. What if I live a long time, how will I support myself in my old age? What if I get sick and become dependent on the charity of others? I must work hard now, and make enough money for the future – and so on. But like a leaky ship, says Evagrius, the person with many possessions is 'awash with his concerns' and runs the risk of being sunk by them.[29] If we wish to be free, we must break out of such snares by embracing radical poverty – freedom from the

---

[29] Evagrius, *Eight Thoughts* 3.3.

delusion of ownership – so that our possessions do not possess us. At the same time, he must also beware of taking pride in his poverty, for the demon of avarice is 'most varied and ingenious in deceit'.[30] For example, the ascetic can be deceived into thinking that it would be good to make lots of money in order to be able to give it to charity; but in so doing, they would make themselves vulnerable to the pitfall of vanity. The demon of avarice thus represents all manner of concern with the empty values and transitory things of the world – both possessions and achievements – in which we invest our sense of self.

Sadness, the fourth of the eight thoughts, is the one that is missing from the seven deadly sins; it got absorbed into sloth. The word in Greek, *lupe*, generally refers to pain – mental and physical – grief, or distress. 'Sadness', says Evagrius, 'involves the frustration of a pleasure, whether actually present or only hoped for'.[31] It is interesting to note that his description of the demon of sadness is remarkably similar to the Buddhist concept of *duhkha*. Both conditions arise as a result of having to do things we do not want to do, not getting what we want, or the wistful memory of better times and our subsequent regrets over their passing. Once these thoughts of the past take hold of the soul, 'they plunge it into sadness with the realization that former things are no more and cannot be again'.[32] It sets its snare wherever we are most attached, and usually follows in the wake of some other thought, such as avarice (in which case it might accompany the loss of possessions), in the aftermath of anger, or indeed any

---

[30] Evagrius, *On Thoughts* 21.
[31] Evagrius, *Praktikos* 19.
[32] Evagrius, *Praktikos* 10.

of the other demons once their deceptions have carried the mind away and abandoned it. Apparently sadness is also sometimes associated with particularly violent demonic attacks, which may even leave physical marks. We would probably call these psychosomatic symptoms today, but I think it noteworthy that Evagrius specifically highlights sadness – rather than any of the other thoughts – given that contemporary medicine so often suggests a link between depression and physical ill health.

Of all the thoughts, anger is probably the one we can most easily associate with being 'possessed'. The literature of the desert fathers, coming out of a world of harsh justice, devotes a great deal of attention to the problem of anger. Indeed, it may come as a surprise to discover that for Evagrius it is not sex but anger that is deemed to be the greatest obstacle in the spiritual life. Anger poisons community spirit and destroys fraternal love. The only time anger can be legitimately expressed is when it is directed against demons, although this can sometimes be a risky strategy as the demons may try to trick a monk in order to provoke him to anger under false pretences. Likening anger to a vicious dog, Evagrius notes that even among the brethren – who have presumably renounced food, wealth, and esteem – anger can very easily be aroused on utterly trivial pretexts, as anyone who has shared a house with friends will undoubtedly know all too well. 'Why do you feed this dog, if you claim to own nothing?' he asks. 'If it barks and attacks people, it is obvious that it has possessions inside and wants to guard them.'[33] Once again Evagrius clearly sees that our behaviour is conditioned by our attachments, not only

---

[33] Evagrius, *On Thoughts* 5.

to things, but also to notions of who and what we think we are: we get angry when our 'possessions' are threatened or compromised.

The next of the thoughts in Evagrius' list is in many ways the most intriguing, for it is the spirit of our age. Acedia is an important technical term in monastic theology, whose meaning is not fully expressed by the word 'sloth' (which is what it becomes in the seven deadly sins). Origen ascribes the original 'Fall' of humanity to the influence of acedia, which he explains not so much in terms of a deliberate act of disobedience, but as a kind of negligence or carelessness with regard to God – rather like an athlete who neglects their training and is subsequently unable to give their best performance. Known as the 'noonday demon' – for it is especially active between 10 am and 2 pm – acedia is the spirit of restless boredom, which may for example be associated with the common but invariably deluded notion that the grass is greener on the other side of the fence. It leads the monk – or indeed us for that matter – to abandon the task at hand, dissatisfied with our apparent lack of progress. Acedia is the tendency to imagine that things were better in the past, or that if only one were to change one's circumstances, then everything would be fine. It is the feeling that what we are doing is a waste of time, and it manifests in the procrastination and displacement activities familiar to anyone who has whiled away an afternoon staring out of the window, or sat at work watching the clock, absent-mindedly checking for emails and surfing the internet. In short, the demon of acedia is the apathy and distractedness so characteristic of modern life. Evagrius describes it perfectly: 'First of all, he makes it appear that the sun moves slowly or not at all, and that the day seems to be fifty hours long. Then he compels the monk to look constantly towards the windows, to jump out of the cell, to watch the sun to see how far it is from the ninth hour, to look this way and that lest one of the brothers . . .'[34] Lest one of the brothers should what?

Anything at all.

The demon of vainglory, which Evagrius defines as the tendency to seek the praise and admiration of other people, can be extremely hard to spot for it will often present itself disguised as a spiritual virtue. It might, for example, cause a monk to imagine himself to be a great teacher, leader or healer, and induce fantasies about being feted by a throng of admirers, or accruing honours and status on account of his good deeds. 'It invents demons crying out, women being healed and a crowd touching his garments; it even predicts to him that he will eventually attain the priesthood. [. . .] When this thought has thus raised him aloft on empty hopes, it flies off abandoning him to be tempted either by the demon of pride or by that of sadness.'[35] All the demons are accompanied by vanity, which waits to step into the breach when another is defeated, tempting the monk with his success, and thus making him vulnerable to the seductions of pride. Indeed, vanity and pride are regarded as the most dangerous of the demons, for they launch their attack only after the other thoughts have been conquered; in other words, when the monk is liable to suppose he is making good progress on the spiritual path. This is why Evagrius likens vanity to a traitor who opens the gates of the city to let the enemy in, and also why it is especially difficult to overcome this demon, as anything that succeeds against it – such as

---

[34] Evagrius, *Praktikos* 12.
[35] Evagrius, *Praktikos* 13.

humility – can all too easily become a further source of vanity. The only remedy is for the monk to guard against this subtle poison until he loses his taste for what the world holds dear.

Closely related to vanity, pride is the most dangerous demon of all, for it induces 'the soul to refuse to acknowledge that God is its helper and to think that it is itself the cause of its good actions'.[36] Anger and sadness invariably follow close on the heels of pride, because pride makes us arrogant and intolerant of those who do not share our view of things. It can even lead to 'the ultimate evil, derangement of mind, madness, and the vision of a multitude of demons in the air'.[37] In order to avoid such a fall, Evagrius counsels the monk to maintain a modest silence with regard to the fruit of his ascetic labours, 'lest unfastened by your tongue they be stolen by esteem'.[38] This high-lights an important point about Christian asceticism: it is not through our own efforts that we advance in spiritual progress. If he wishes to avoid the snare of pride, the monk must never forget that the strength he has for ascetic practice comes from God alone, who is the ultimate source of all that is good and true; while 'everything that goes to excess comes from the demons'.[39] This is precisely why the monastic tradition is so adamant that one must only engage in those austerities that are prescribed, and submit to the authority of a trusted guide. I know from my own limited experience how easily one can be tempted by pride to try and be more 'spiritual' than others, maybe by getting up earlier, meditating for longer, or eating less.

---

[36] Evagrius, *Praktikos* 14.
[37] Evagrius, *Praktikos* 14.
[38] Evagrius, *Eulogios* 14.
[39] *Alphabetical Collection* Poemen 129.

Having classified the thoughts, what next? Demons work by manipulating the mind's mental objects – memories in other words – so therefore, by carefully noting the thoughts that arise, the monk is able to identify the demon responsible. This requires the monk to cultivate a high degree of self-awareness or mindfulness, in order to see which of the eight obsessive thoughts is at work. Interestingly, Evagrius says that we have no control over whether these thoughts come to afflict us, but we are able to decide whether or not they stay to affect us. Succumbing to the influence of *logismoi* results from a failure to exercise right discrimination; therefore the monk must learn to discern whether a thought is angelic or demonic, which demons do what, the company they keep, the relationships between them, and the circumstances in which they appear.

Evagrius describes the practice of discerning thoughts/demons in some detail. First of all, our mental activity must be closely observed so that each thought can be analysed down to its four component parts. These are: the perceiving mind, the object it is thinking of, the mental image of that object and the feeling it induces. Evagrius points out that the mind is the image of God, physical objects are morally neutral, and the mental image likewise, so therefore it must be the fourth element – the thought or feeling induced – that is the source of the soul's disturbance. Thus by distinguishing these various factors from each other, the monk is able to see things the way they are: that it is neither the mind in itself, nor the physical world that is the problem, but rather that there is a demon at work. At this point the unwholesome thought will simply dissipate, no longer able to hold the mind in its thrall. Thoughts are, after all, only thoughts. Importantly, this is not just a solitary pursuit: it requires expert guidance. Careful introspection is complemented with what can be best described as 'counselling sessions' with the master, which – over fifteen-hundred years before Freud – would often include the interpretation of dreams.

Having identified the thought, and thus the relevant 'demon', the monk must then learn how to counteract it in order to be free of its influence on his behaviour. Demons are, however, deceptive by nature, constantly changing the forms in which they present themselves. For example, they might praise the ascetic, in order to inspire presumption, leading to vanity and pride; or otherwise belittle his efforts so as to induce hopelessness and despair. This obviously makes the task of discernment very difficult so Evagrius offers detailed advice, noting for example that one cannot be attacked by two demons at the same time, because the mind cannot conceive of two mental objects or thoughts at the same time. He then suggests various crafty tips, such as how to play one demon off against another, since some – such as vanity and lust – are mutually incompatible: after all, the former promises honours, while the latter leads to dishonour.

Evagrius even warns us about what we can expect as we engage in this practice. The first line of attack always involves the demons of gluttony, avarice, and vainglory. Once the mind has been breached by one of these thoughts, the rest follow close behind. In order to resist this first wave of attack, the monk must engage in fasting, charity and earnest prayer so as to cultivate detachment from food, riches and esteem (roughly corresponding to our contemporary idols of sex, money, and power). Reciting the psalms is commended for its calming effect, and Evagrius talks about responding to the attacks of specific demons or thoughts with appropriate passages from scripture, citing the temptation of Jesus in the wilderness as the prototype. This is when the devil tries to engage Jesus in an interior dialogue – tempting him with gluttony, avarice and vainglory – in order to snare him in webs of fantasy and delusion. After all, the 'devil' (from *diabolos*, literally to throw across), manifests as whatever it is that possesses the mind or stands between us and who we really are – the obstruction in our path. Jesus simply refuses to get involved, responding instead with sharp bolts of scripture to silence the unwelcome intruder.[40] For this reason Evagrius recommends simple prayers, such as 'Lord have mercy', which can either be uttered as quick darts to repel an unwholesome thought, or repeated continuously like a mantra.

After learning to recognize the basic activities of the thoughts, the monk is then taught to discern some of the more subtle tactics that demons might deploy. For instance, when the demon of gluttony fails to turn the monk from his abstinence, it may change tack and instead goad him to an even more severe asceticism, 'so that in pursuing an immoderate abstinence he may fail to attain even a moderate one, the body not being strong enough because of its weakness'.[41] This is a good example of how devious the mind can be in playing tricks on us. It also highlights the fact that, contrary to the popular stereotype, monastic asceticism is not about repressing the body: it has nothing to do with masochistic self-hatred, but rather is concerned with loving God. Its aim is to turn our appetites for sensual pleasure into desire for (knowledge of) God, and our passions

---

[40] Matthew 4.1–11.
[41] Evagrius, *On Thoughts* 35.

into hatred of demons and aversion to evil. Indeed the purpose of discerning thoughts, or identifying these demons, is to enable the monk to know better the virtues that need to be cultivated in order to effect that transformation, so that ultimately the soul may realize its true nature as made in the image of God.

CHAPTER SIX

Benedict

I n the early fifth century, the tranquillity of the Egyptian wilderness was rudely shattered as marauding Berber tribes took advantage of the weakness of the Roman Empire. The monastic settlement of Scetis was sacked by raiders in 407, less than eighty years after its foundation by Macarius the Great, and many of those who did not manage to escape were killed. Like the fleeting bloom of a desert flower, the first phase of Christian monasticism was coming to an end, and although some monks returned, none of the leading figures of its heyday were among them. The site was sacked again several times over the next few decades, and all but abandoned following the Muslim conquests of the seventh century. But the monastic spirit was never completely extinguished and today there are four Coptic monasteries in the Wadi Natrun area, south of Alexandria. All of them ancient foundations – three dating back to the earliest settlements, a fourth founded in the eighth century – they have recently undergone extensive reconstruction, and now house thriving communities of contemporary desert monks.

Fortunately, the ascetic tradition of the desert had started to put down roots in the west long before the demise of Scetis. Athanasius' *Life of Antony* was already an international bestseller, and throughout the fifth century works relating to Egyptian monasticism were being translated into Latin almost as soon as they appeared in the original Greek. By far the most important figure in this transmission was undoubtedly John Cassian (c. 360–c. 435), the only desert father to have written in Latin, whose principal works – namely the *Institutes* and the *Conferences* – were composed with the express purpose of making the teachings of the Egyptian monks available to the fledgling monastic communities of Europe.

We know relatively little about Cassian himself; we do not even have the benefit of a hagiography to sift for snippets of information. Drawing such biographical details as they can from his writings, scholars speculate that he may originally have come from Scythia, an area of modern day Romania, which would account for his fluency in both Latin and Greek. Travelling to the Holy Land as a pilgrim, he became a monk in Bethlehem in about 380, before going on to Egypt in the mid-380s to live among the monks of Nitria and Scetis. He remained there until 399 when Theophilus, who had succeeded Athanasius as patriarch of Alexandria, instigated a violent reaction against the teachings of Origen, forcing many monks to leave Egypt.

The trouble started when, in his festal letter announcing the date of Easter, Theophilus also took the opportunity to promote Origen's teachings on the incorporeality of God by condemning anthropomorphism, the tendency to attribute human characteristics to the Divine. The letter provoked a hostile split between Origenists and anthropomorphites, poignantly expressed – in Cassian's account – by the elderly monk Serapion, who on hearing the letter broke down in tears crying: 'They have taken my God from me, and I have no one to lay hold of, nor do I know whom I should adore or address.'[42]

---

[42] Boniface Ramsey (trans.), *John Cassian: The Conferences* (New York: Newman Press, 1997), p. 373.

Following a massive protest by the anthropomorphites, Theophilus reversed his earlier position and instead condemned the teachings of Origen, whose adherents – Cassian among them – were hounded out of their monasteries. Going first to Constantinople, where he was ordained by John Chrysostom, and then on to Rome, Cassian eventually settled in southern Gaul near present-day Marseilles. Here he founded two monasteries, and in the 420s composed the works for which he is now known.

Cassian was clearly a follower of Evagrius, although he never mentions him by name due to the latter's association with the controversial Origen. Nevertheless, Cassian wholeheartedly adopts the Evagrian scheme of the stages of the ascetic life (which he renders as purgation, illumination and union), and like Evagrius, he places particular emphasis on the discernment of thoughts. Although scholars may debate the extent to which Cassian's writings – which purport to relate conversations with the monks of the desert – are historically factual or simply a convenient literary form in which to express his own theology, the significance of these texts to the development of western monasticism cannot be overemphasized. Indeed, his works are still read in monasteries to this day.

Nearly sixteen-hundred years later, my own – admittedly rather different – sojourn among the wise men of the east drew to a close when one day Swami Krishnananda said something that made me think it was time to go home. It may have been when he asked me, once again, what I was doing there; or perhaps he said something about England that somehow just pressed a button. Whatever it was, it felt like a clear hint. I had been away nearly two years, was more or less out of money, and had in any case always known that at some point I would inevitably have to leave. By the time I arrived back in the UK I had nothing but a $100 bill in my pocket and a change of clothing. I had no bank account and nowhere to live; I wasn't registered with a doctor, and I hadn't paid any taxes for almost ten years. In short, I had more or less disappeared from the system. But far more important than any of this, I was a completely different person: I didn't drink, and I believed in God – more or less. These two facts meant that everything about my life before I went away – my old friends, my familiar haunts – was now alien to me. It was as if I had been born anew, and I had to start from scratch.

While I had been away, I had also come to realize that I was not a Buddhist. During the course of my stay with the Thai monks in New Zealand, I got to know the visiting French monk Ajahn Thitanano quite well, and was able to learn a great deal from his knowledge and experience of Buddhism. It was somehow easier to talk to him than the Thai monks, perhaps because we had more in common culturally. In our lively conversations, however, I also encountered a frustrated Roman Catholic adolescent who had never managed to get beyond the authoritarian God of his childhood. And that made me think. What if his understanding of the religion he had adopted was as literal-minded as his understanding of the one he had rejected? I began to see that a religion is not just an abstract set of beliefs and practices, existing in isolation from the rest of human culture, but – like the language we speak – part of the very fabric of who and what we are. Just as Ajahn Thitanano would never cease to be French, so he would always be someone who had been formed in a Christian culture. In his case, that seemed to be a source of tension – between what he had been and what he had become – though admittedly it might not be so for everybody. Nevertheless, I could see the potential for a similar tension within myself, and so as a result of this insight, I intuitively felt it made more sense to try and play the hand that the circumstances of life had dealt me, rather than 'shopping around' for the spirituality that suited me.

For the first few months following my return to England I was slightly at a loss as to what I should do with myself. After two years absolutely free of all commitments and responsibilities, it was initially quite difficult to get back into normal life. I instinctively knew I wanted somehow to continue the spiritual journey I had begun in India and with the Buddhists, but did not really know how to go about it as a Christian and in a western society. I did not want to join a religious order, so much as find a way of being a monk in everyday life. I continued to meditate of course, but slowly, bit by bit, the world took hold of me again.

Within a year I had a job, a car, a mortgage and a handful of credit cards. I was in a relationship and, for the first time ever, wearing a tie to work. You can give up the world, but that does not necessarily mean it has given up on you. I found it all somewhat bemusing really, because I didn't try to make any of this happen; it all just came about on its own. But as I got more involved in the affairs of the world, so the single-pointed clarity of mind that I had experienced while living a more or less monastic life slowly began to fade. I tried to find out about communities in Britain, but the religious life of this country tends to be somewhat hidden, and I was essentially an outsider. One day, however, flicking through various religious reference books and directories in my local public library, I made the pleasing discovery that there were communities of monks and nuns in the Church of England. Indeed, there happened to be a monastery very close to where I was then living. That afternoon, I telephoned to ask if it would be possible to pay them a visit.

"Certainly! Come for tea on Sunday. It's at four o'clock."

A few days later, I cycled over to the monastery of Elmore Abbey, a community of Anglican Benedictines founded in 1914. Initially I thought I had made a mistake and gone to the wrong address; it didn't look much like a monastery. But then the door opened and I was greeted by a man in a black habit who could not have been anything other than a monk. The Abbot showed me round, I attended a short service, and stayed for a very English cup of tea and a slice of rather good homemade cake. Before leaving, I asked the Abbot if it would be okay to visit again, perhaps on a regular basis. He agreed, and so nearly every day for the next three years I went to the evening office of vespers, which was followed by a period of silent meditation. I eventually became an Oblate of the community – a sort of associate member – with a rule of life and a commitment to the principles of Benedictine discipleship.

In Benedict I found a kindred spirit. Like us, he lived in a violent, unstable age. Like me, he was a high-school dropout. The biography written by Gregory the Great in about 593 may leave the modern reader frustrated for want of reliable historical information, but Gregory's primary concern was to write a hagiography extolling the virtues of a saint, and as such it served its purpose well. *The Life of St Benedict*, full of fantastic miracle stories, was one of the most popular books of the middle ages. From it we can surmise that Benedict (*c.* 480–547) was born into a well-to-do family in Nursia, a town about one hundred miles northeast of Rome, during the turbulent dying days of the western Roman empire, as Europe entered what came to be known as the 'dark ages'.

The history of fifth-century Rome is a story of perpetual warfare, famine and economic instability. The city first fell to Alaric the Visigoth in 410, and was sacked again in 455, this time by the Vandals. For the next twenty years, a succession of weak emperors, often dominated by their foreign generals, struggled to retain control over what was left of the once extensive Roman dominions. As one territory after another was ceded to nominally vassal kings, all that remained under imperial jurisdiction was basically just Italy itself. In 476, just four years before Benedict was born, the last emperor Romulus was deposed in a coup led by his own army and replaced by the Germanic general Odoacer.

War broke out again in 489 when Theodoric, king of the Ostrogoths, invaded Italy on behalf of the Byzantine emperor, Zeno. Emerging victorious in 493, Theodoric ruled Italy until 526, during which time Rome enjoyed a period of relative stability. The new king, who never sought the title 'emperor', was a great admirer of Roman culture, and an enthusiastic patron of the arts and learning. During his reign he made a point of trying to keep the imperial administration intact, even going so far as to reinstate a number of ancient institutions that had fallen into abeyance. The Roman senate remained in place, as did all the machinery of the law and taxation, and Roman citizens continued to occupy civil offices. However, after the death of Theodoric's grandson and successor, Athalaric, war broke out again in 535 when the new Byzantine emperor, Justinian, invaded Italy and waged a protracted and bloody campaign against the Ostrogoths that lasted until 553.

Roman society at this time combined elements of the pagan past with the more recent influence of the now dominant Christian church. Although pagan and Christian morals probably had a lot more in common than one might at first imagine, differences of emphasis in certain areas meant that Christian values were sometimes at odds with existing practices. For example, the public baths – an immensely popular social institution – were censured by the church for being conducive to lascivious conduct, although this injunction seems to have been disregarded by all, including it would appear, the clergy themselves. On the whole, pagan society had been rather more relaxed about sex: concubines were a normal feature of everyday life, prostitution was legal, and divorce by consent – at the instigation of either party – was common. The church, on the other hand, decreed that all sex outside marriage was sinful and only sanctioned divorce in cases of proven adultery. Once again however, the church's official pronouncements do not seem to have had much impact on established customs. In spite of various laws restricting divorce, it remained prevalent – even among Christians – throughout this period. A similar account can be given of prostitution, which was legally licensed and taxed up until the middle of the fifth century. Although it was eventually banned, the law seems to have been blatantly ignored, and business continued as usual.

Despite the fact that most people in Roman society were by now Christian, the church was still feeling its way through the transition from underground millenarian sect to institutionalized state religion. Thus Christians continued to be discouraged from serving in the army or the administration, even though the church was rapidly becoming an important part of the socio-political establishment.

The struggle to reconcile Christian morals with existing cultural norms that were essentially pagan in origin became particularly acute with regard to the games – the great public entertainments consisting of chariot races, wild animal hunts, gladiators and drama. Christians were staunchly opposed to the games on principle, due to their historical links to pagan cults; and gladiator shows – which were basically organized murder – predictably drew severe condemnation. Perhaps surprisingly, however, theatrical entertainments were, if anything, even more strongly criticized on account of their frequently lewd content. Indeed, the entertainment industry was held in such low regard that actors and actresses were barred from membership of the church unless they renounced their licentious profession. Although the gladiators had been successfully banned by Constantine – long before Benedict's time – wild animal hunts, racing, and dramatic performances continued. Chariot racing, in particular, was hugely popular. Fans were split into the Blues and the Greens; loyalties were fierce and rioting frequent. Broadly speaking, ordinary Roman citizens were Romans first of all, and Christians second.

Church leaders may have wished it were otherwise, but the fact is that the coming of Christianity does not appear to have resulted in a more godly society. In spite of the threat of eternal damnation, there is even evidence to suggest that in some respects public morality actually *declined* under the Christian emperors of the fourth and fifth centuries. The indiscriminate use of torture and flogging became more common, and brutal sentences – such as burning alive – were imposed for an increasingly wide range of offences. Administrative and judicial corruption also seem to have worsened. Ironically, this may have been something to do with the great surge in the popularity of monasticism during the fifth and sixth centuries, as Christians extolled the virtue of renunciation over public service. The fact is, monasticism in the west was still at this early stage a movement that was largely inspired by books – such as *The Life of Antony*, and the works of Cassian, Jerome, and Palladius – so it primarily appealed to the educated classes. In other words, the people attracted to monasticism – educated and virtuous – were precisely those who might otherwise have been expected to take up careers in the imperial administration. Instead, disillusioned with the state of the world and despairing of ever being able to lead a sinless Christian life amid the decadence and corruption of the city, these idealistic young men and women turned their backs on society and fled to the countryside, pledging themselves to lives of prayer and the study of scripture.

Sometime at the end of the fifth century, the young Benedict is supposed to have enrolled as a student in Rome. The standard academic programme, inherited largely unchanged from antiquity, would have consisted of the study of grammar and rhetoric, and the works of classical authors, such as Virgil and Cicero, together with commentaries on the historical, mythological or geographical allusions contained therein. The notion of 'research', so fundamental to the modern academy, would have been un-heard of; scholarship in this period amounted to little more than memorizing a fixed canon of knowledge. An educated man, therefore, was one who could write elegant letters, dash off a few lines of passable verse and pepper their conversation with erudite trivia. For Christians who believed that the Bible – replete with cultural as well as spiritual treasures – was the only book anyone ever needed to read, such a syllabus might have been hard to swallow, and many were wary of reading pagan authors. Jerome's nightmare, in which he finds himself before the throne of judgement accused of being a Ciceronian rather than a Christian, captures this sentiment perfectly. Having said that, in practice most people accepted that reading the pagan classics was necessary if one wanted to be educated at all, and many prominent and highly cultivated public figures, such as the senator Boethius, were also, of course, Christians.

Benedict did not remain a student for long. It seems he was absolutely appalled by the loose morals and fast living of the student lifestyle he encountered in Rome. Aged twenty, we are told, he abandoned his studies and left the city to go and live in a cave near Subiaco, some sixty miles away. It is perhaps not insignificant to note that in the year 500, when Benedict is supposed to have dropped out of college, the most lavish and magnificent games the city had seen in decades were staged in honour of King Theodoric's triumphal state visit to Rome. After so many years of war and its attendant miseries, one can just imagine the streets awash with drunken revellers as the people of Rome abandoned themselves to wild, uninhibited partying. Perhaps it was all too much for Benedict who, repelled by the futility of a life devoted solely to hedonism, turned away in disgust to seek the eternal truth in prayer and solitude.

But that was then and this is now, you might be thinking. Things have changed a bit in the last fifteen-hundred years. Or have they? Although one should be wary of drawing simplistic parallels between vastly different historical periods, the situation we are in today does seem to have at least something in common with Europe at the dawn of the middle ages. Post-imperial political and economic instability afflict many parts of our world; and, just like the Romans, we too are completely addicted to entertainment. In Benedict's era it was the circus; today we have the gladiatorial arena of reality TV shows, where we can voyeuristically watch people tearing each other apart. In the ancient world entertainments were sacred, perhaps because of a belief that games of chance mirrored – and thus might, by analogy, influence – the vagaries of the cosmos. Many sacred sites, such as the famous temple complex at Delphi, also included a theatre and a stadium, emphasizing the intimate relationship between sacred ritual, drama and games. Little has changed, except that now it is more difficult to tell the difference between them. As churches try to be more 'entertaining', the entertainment industry is becoming the primary channel for contemporary religiosity, football fans have an almost religious devotion to their team, and celebrities are worshipped and adored as if they were deities.

Gregory tells us that Benedict composed a *Rule* for his monks 'remarkable for its discretion', and further, that if anyone should want to know more about his character or way of life they should read it, for he was such a man as could not teach other than as he lived.[43] Benedict probably composed the *Rule* sometime between 530 and 540 while he was Abbot of Monte Cassino, the monastery he founded in about 529.[44] In it he stresses the importance of obedience and the authority of the Abbot, which was to be absolute, even to

---

[43] Carolinne White (trans.), *Early Christian Lives* (London: Penguin Books, 1998), p. 202.

[44] Extracts from the Rule of St Benedict (RB) taken from the English translation in Timothy Fry (ed.), *The Rule of St Benedict in English* (Collegeville, Minnesota: Liturgical Press, 1982).

the extent that monks should – if possible – obey an impossible order.[45] The *Rule* envisages a strictly hierarchical and tightly controlled community, whose contact with the world beyond the cloister walls is severely limited. Like the desert fathers, to whom it is likely Benedict looked for inspiration, the discipline he seeks to inculcate is based on withdrawal from the concerns of everyday life, in order to cultivate silence, obedience, and humility. But he was not simply an imitator. With his emphasis on corporate monasticism as the normative model, and his more relaxed attitude towards asceticism compared with the desert fathers, Benedict shows a sensitivity to context that resulted in the emergence of a distinctively western monastic tradition.

Benedict's strong emphasis on authority probably also reflects something of his cultural and historical circumstances. He was, after all, a Roman citizen, and the *Rule* reflects a very Roman predilection for written legislation. It should come as no surprise therefore, to discover that for Benedict a monk is by definition someone whose life is governed by a code of law, hence the 'regular' life: life lived according to a rule. Likewise, given the restless, insecure times in which he lived, we might expect Benedict to have a particular concern for stability, which must have been one of the major issues of the day. Both these elements are plainly evident in the instructions for receiving novices into the monastery: the prospective brother is to promise 'perseverance in his stability' and agree to live under the law of the *Rule*.[46] He is then to have the *Rule* read through to him on two more occasions over a period adding up to a year,

---

[45] RB 68.1.
[46] RB 58.9.

before making a commitment for life. At this point 'he comes before the whole community in the oratory and promises stability, fidelity to the monastic life, and obedience'.[47] This then is Benedict's prescription for those who wish 'to do battle for Christ' in the 'school for the Lord's service'.[48]

One further point to bear in mind when thinking about the *Rule* is that even as late as the sixth century, a monastery could very often simply be someone's house, and the community a small informal group of like-minded souls experimenting with an alternative lifestyle. In other words, monasticism was not the highly developed institution with which we are now familiar, and monks and nuns were not the special class of 'religious professionals' that we might now see them as. It was for example the exception rather than the norm for monks to be ordained. In Benedict's day, priests were only admitted reluctantly, and on condition that they submit to the *Rule* like everybody else, expecting no preferential treatment on account of their rank.[49] The *Rule* is not therefore a manual for spiritual experts; nor is it meant to be an exhaustive guide to the minutiae of a regulated life. Monasteries had to draw up detailed constitutions precisely for that purpose. It is rather a set of simple, practical guidelines for ordinary men and women seeking to live authentic gospel-based lives, and as such it contains much that is relevant and useful to us living in the world today.

Perhaps this helps explain the fact that Benedictine spirituality currently seems to be enjoying such a vibrant renaissance, as indicated

---

[47] RB 58.17.
[48] RB Prologue 45.
[49] RB 60.

by the plethora of books on the subject, and widespread media interest in retreats and meditation. Indeed, Benedict's star has been quietly rising since 1980 when Pope John Paul II made him patron saint of Europe; and it is surely no coincidence that his successor took the name of Benedict XVI when he was elected in 2005, declaring that the re-evangelization of Europe would be the priority of his papacy. Along with many other religious leaders, the Pope has been outspoken in his criticisms of the culture of relativism afflicting contemporary society, arguing that our standards of conduct and behaviour are no longer determined by reference to any objective measure of right and wrong, but appear to be based simply on personal preferences. The result is a society that attaches great value to the accumulation of power, possessions and wealth. The ability to do whatever we want, whenever we want to do it, has become all-important; and we expect to be able to indulge our every whim and fancy – preferably instantly. Yet far from being conducive to human flourishing, such narcissistic life-goals are ultimately dehumanizing, rendering us objects as well as agents of consumption. We commonly believe that freedom of choice is the highest good; Benedict, by contrast, tells us that if we wish to be truly free, we must 'hate the urgings of self-will'.[50]

My initial encounters with monasticism – Buddhist, Hindu, and Christian – had made me feel as if I was being who and what I was really meant to be. There was something about the religious life, its singularity of purpose, that was very compelling to me. But I needed to find a way of doing and being that in the world. Without any clear idea of what I hoped to find there, I decided to start going to church.

---

[50] RB 4.60.

CHAPTER SEVEN

A Little Rule for Beginners

My first experience of attending church in Britain as an adult appalled me, and I was very tempted to quit straight away. I am not sure why the Church of England is so spiritually lacklustre; but whatever the reason, rather like decaf coffee, there is just something not quite right about it. Two or three weeks later I gave it another try, determined to make a go of the Christian thing. I wanted a story that I could feel properly at home in, that I could identify with at some sort of gut level. But I found it very hard to relate to what went on in church – which seemed both familiar and alien at the same time – and I had completely forgotten how grimly tedious, contrived and banal it could sometimes be. I needed to talk to someone, so I asked the vicar if we could have a chat. When we met a few days later, I surprised myself by telling him I felt called to be a priest. I could hardly believe my own ears – it was as if I was confessing a guilty secret – and I was very cautious about mentioning it to anybody else. But the more I thought about it, the more it made sense. It seemed like the ideal way of being a monk in the world: a full-time religious professional – praying for a living, as it were – but still very much involved in society. Having set in motion a process that almost immediately took on a life of its own, I wrote a letter to my local bishop, and started to read the Christian mystics.

I was put in touch with a vocations advisor who told me I needed to get involved in parish life, and demonstrate a bit of stability – perhaps by showing I could hold down a job. This was not quite what I wanted to hear, although admittedly it was to be expected. After all, I had just turned up out of the blue, knew next to nothing about the church, and was not even sure I was really doing the right thing. There seemed to be such a gulf between what I understood as the spiritual life, and what went on in church on a Sunday morning, and I had little confidence I would make it through the selection process. So I made a backup plan, just in case. All the reading I had done while I had been away had given me a taste for learning, making me think it would be a good idea to go to university in order to continue the studies I had already begun on my own. It was not that I doubted I had a vocation – there was no question that I had to somehow be in the 'religion business' – it just was not immediately clear what form this would take. If it's not going to be the priesthood, I reasoned, then perhaps I can be an academic theologian.

The only problem with this idea was that I didn't have the grades. School had not been a great success. In those days, I had absolutely no interest in higher education: my only ambition was to play in a band. When in my early thirties I changed my mind, I had to take evening classes to gain the necessary entry qualifications. Without any real expectation of success, but being persuaded that I had nothing to lose, I thought I would try for Oxbridge. Initial enquiries were not well received: I was bluntly told that my academic record did not match the 'typical profile'. One college, however, said that although my CV was a little unusual, if I put in an application they would take a look at it. I did, they did, and in 1999 – fifteen years after being expelled from two schools for making bombs, taking drugs, and generally not playing enough rugby – I went to Cambridge to study theology, staying on to do a master's degree and then a doctorate.

I ended up doing my PhD on the Buddhist doctrine of emptiness, or *sunyata*. The prospect of writing eighty thousand words on nothing should have been enough to put anyone off – everything. Just before I began my research, I suffered a major loss of confidence. This is probably something anyone might expect when undertaking a major project, except that in my case it was not only an uncertainty about my ability to do the job – though I obviously felt that too – but a lack of commitment to the subject on a personal level. I had, in other words, a crisis of faith: I began to doubt my doubts. The Buddha steadfastly maintained that he taught two things, and two things only: that life sucks, and that there is something we can do about it. He was absolutely adamant that it was pointless to ask speculative metaphysical questions – such as whether or not the universe is eternal, whether or not the soul is separate from the body, and so on – because we will be dead long before we get a conclusive answer. He skilfully rebutted anyone who attempted to draw him out on these matters, saying that such knowledge was not necessary – or even useful – to the immediate task at hand: the problem of *duhkha*. As far as it goes, this is fair enough. It would seem perfectly reasonable to suggest that there is no point seeking answers to unanswerable questions. Buddhism has a logic and a coherence that is very compelling, and it is surely no accident that a kind of 'implicit Buddhism' permeates the default worldview of so many people in contemporary secular societies. If the Buddhists are right in claiming that questions concerning the origin and final destiny of things are irrelevant, then that is the end of the matter. Yet the fact is we do ask these questions. What if it is the very asking of the question – not whether it can be answered – that is the point? If this is the case, then the Buddhist position would seem to be ultimately unsatisfactory. If there is any point in asking a question that cannot be answered – because it is the question itself that matters – then I needed to reconsider my position.

Six months into my doctoral research, and becoming increasingly disillusioned by it, I received a forwarded email from a television company looking for volunteers to spend forty days in a monastery. Without really giving it a second thought, I responded immediately, remembering how much I had enjoyed the experience of living in religious communities almost a decade earlier. It sounded like the opportunity I did not realize I needed, a chance to get myself back on track, pointing towards what really matters. When I told friends about the project, most of them – knowing that I'm 'well up for a bit of monking' – were not at all surprised that I had volunteered, although thanks to the influence of all those reality TV shows we love to hate, some were rather sceptical about the integrity of the venture. To be honest, so was I. But it was not until the day I was due to depart for the monastery that I suddenly realized it may have been a little rash to put myself at the mercy of a TV production company. What if they wanted to make some tacky reality show out of it? What if the other guys turned out to be really difficult to get along with? In spite of being reassured that it was going to be a serious documentary, it was not until I actually got to the monastery and talked to some of the monks – who of course had also put their own necks on the block – that I felt confident it was going to be okay. After all, I reasoned, they are monks: they would not have gotten themselves into this without thinking it through *very* carefully!

The stated aim of this 'unique experiment', in which a group of five men were to spend six weeks living alongside a community of Benedictine monks, was to see whether there was anything about the monastic tradition that might be relevant to modern life. The resulting programme, screened in May 2005 and simply called *The Monastery*, turned out to be an unexpected success, which took many people by surprise – including the programme's makers. Judged to be both sensitive and intelligent – not descriptions usually associated with the genre of reality TV – for a few weeks it provoked extensive discussion in the media. Worth Abbey, the monastery in question, received hundreds of letters and emails, testimony to the profound impact the programme had on people from all walks of life, believers and non-believers alike. In today's allegedly secular society, religious people are often seen as being a bit odd – at best – so it is all the more significant to note that one of the most frequently made comments about the programme was how balanced and normal the monks appeared to be, especially when compared with their visitors from the so-called 'normal' world.

So what's the attraction? Why would anyone willingly exchange the comfort and freedom of their everyday life for the austerity and self-denial of a monastery? How would we cope without all the things we would be forced to give up? Predictably, the first thing the monks needed to teach us was to live according to the rhythm and discipline of their highly regimented life. For many people, discipline is a word that tends to conjure up negative connotations of punishment and repression, but we should remember that 'discipline' is related to discipleship, and in ordinary language we also use it to refer to a skill or training. Although it may look excessively austere to us, monastic discipline should be understood as a middle way, neither repressive nor indulgent. This is well illustrated by the advice given to Evagrius by his teacher Macarius, who said that a monk should live each day ready to die on the morrow, and yet at the same time take care of his body as if he would be living with it for many years to come.[51] Likewise, Benedict maintains that his *Rule* contains 'nothing harsh, nothing burdensome', but that at the same time a little strictness may be necessary, for the good of all, since the road to salvation is 'bound to be narrow at the outset'.[52]

From this it is clear that Benedict believes discipline is absolutely fundamental to any meaningful transformation. Monks, by definition, 'no longer live by their own judgement, giving in to their whims and appetites; rather they walk according to another's decisions and directions, choosing to live in monasteries and have an abbot over them'.[53] Far from being restrictive, however, it is precisely the shared discipline of the rule that enables people who may otherwise have little in common to live alongside one another in relative harmony. The truth of this becomes all too clear when one member of a group – whether we are talking about a religious community, a sports team, a family or a committee – starts doing their own thing without considering the impact it might have on everybody else. Left unchecked their egocentricity will eventually destroy the group altogether. And yet, far from seeing discipline as

---

[51] Evagrius, *Praktikos* 29.
[52] RB Prologue 46–8.
[53] RB 5.12.

'the road to salvation', we are more likely to think of it as something that entails the absence of freedom. Interestingly, the problem here is not that we do not understand the need for discipline – we have no trouble with discipline when it concerns something we want to do – but rather that we do not understand the nature of freedom.

We tend to think that freedom means freedom of choice, even though we often find that the reverse is true. Far from being a recipe for happiness, having more choice can be suffocating and result in an inability to choose, while keeping one's options open brings not freedom but insecurity. Too much choice makes us feel helpless and inadequate, afraid of missing out on other alternatives; it leads not to freedom but paralysis, frustration and despair. Like sleepwalkers in a hallucinatory virtual world of shadows, we live our lives controlled and conditioned, at one remove (at least) from reality. Even our dreams cannot be called our own. Strange as it may initially seem, freedom is actually defined by what limits it. After all, it is the 'narrow gate' that leads to fullness of life,[54] suggesting that the limitation of choice opens up the possibility of a much more expansive freedom. To give an example, although improvising jazz musicians might sound completely anarchic, they are still playing within the constraints and discipline of mutually understood musical conventions. Paradoxically then, discipline is actually the basis of freedom, or in this case, is what marks the difference between music and an unpleasant cacophony.

In common with any discipline, monastic asceticism has a simple rationality: the sacrifice of present enjoyment for the sake of a greater

---

[54] Matthew 7.13, Cf. RB Prologue.

reward in the future. When Benedict says that the monk should embrace suffering and endure it 'without weakening or seeking escape', this is because he can confidently expect his reward from God.[55] Anyone who has studied for an examination, gone on a diet or trained in order to get fit, is already familiar with the basic principle of asceticism; indeed the word *ascesis* originally referred specifically to athletic training. In spiritual terms we might describe asceticism as the deliberate effort to restrain – or perhaps retrain – our worldly appetites for the sake of the knowledge of God. The first monks sought by means of self-mortification to emulate the Christian martyrs of the second- and third-century persecutions. Athanasius tells us about Antony's practice of 'dying daily', and such imagery was frequently adopted by the desert fathers, who saw their asceticism as a 'spiritual martyrdom'. Macarius told a brother who came to him asking for 'a word' that he should 'become a dead man', indifferent to both praise and blame alike.[56] Indeed, until relatively recently Coptic Orthodox monks – heirs of the desert fathers – would be buried without a requiem service because they believed that their 'funeral' had already taken place on the day they were consecrated as monks.

Contrary to what people often imagine, being a monk is not about punishing the body for the sake of it. The desert fathers were quite explicit about this, asserting that it was their obsessions, compulsions and attachments – not their bodies – that needed to be 'killed'. Indeed, the strong emphasis in all monastic traditions on

---

[55] RB 7.39.
[56] *Alphabetical Collection* Macarius 23.

caring for the sick would seem to suggest that a healthy body is considered essential to spiritual wellbeing. An anonymous desert hermit likened the body to a coat, which if looked after will last a long time, but if neglected will fall to pieces.[57] After all, if one's asceticism is too extreme it will end up being physically harmful, thus making it impossible to maintain any kind of spiritual practice whatsoever. This point is well illustrated in a story about a hunter who was shocked when he came across Antony relaxing with some of his monks. In order to show that discipline is about balance not repression, Antony asked the hunter to draw his bow and shoot an arrow. The hunter did so, and then Antony asked him to do it again. And again. Finally the hunter protested: 'If I bend my bow so much I will break it.' Antony replied, 'It is the same with the work of God. If we stretch the brethren beyond measure they will soon break.'[58]

Excessive austerity can be dangerous in other ways too: drawing attention to oneself through displays of extreme asceticism suggests pride rather than piety, and the literature of the desert is full of stories about monks being publicly rebuked for making an exhibition of their feats of self-denial. The role of the Abbot therefore is not only to impose discipline where needed, but also to prevent individual zeal from getting out of hand and becoming a vain ego-trip. Benedict was quite explicit about the dangerous tendency towards 'presumption and vainglory' that could arise from self-directed asceticism.[59] Thus the cultivation of self-awareness, or purifying the soul, requires

---

[57] *Systematic Collection* Lust 40.
[58] *Alphabetical Collection* Antony 13.
[59] RB 49.9, Cf. 7.55.

a balanced discipline; it should not be excessive, although a degree of strictness is also necessary, rather like pruning a plant in order to stimulate its growth.

Benedictine discipline is not about being compelled to do things we don't want to do; it is not rigid and oppressive, but recognizing that people are different, it is characterized by an enlightened spirit of flexibility and balance. Monks should be as capable of enjoying the feast as enduring the fast. This is demonstrated in Benedict's stipulation that a choice of two dishes should be provided at each meal, so that everyone is able to eat something they prefer.[60] He shows a similar attitude regarding the consumption of alcohol, revealing both his continuity with the Egyptian tradition and at the same time his departure from it. Citing Abba Poemen, he says: 'We read that monks should not drink wine at all, but since the monks of our day cannot be convinced of this, let us at least agree to drink moderately, and not to the point of excess.'[61] Once again, recognizing that people are different, he is reluctant to prescribe the 'proper amount', but as a general rule of thumb, and while noting the need to make allowance for individual circumstances and seasonal variations, he suggests that half a bottle per day should be about right.

If it is not viewed as being repressive and masochistic, then the other popular stereotype regarding monasticism is that it is a bit of a soft option: as long as they toe the line, monks and nuns can enjoy a carefree life without any of the worries and responsibilities that afflict the rest of us. From my own experience, I think it would be more

---

[60] RB 39.2.
[61] RB 40.6 (Cf. *Alphabetical Collection* Poemen 19).

accurate to say that a monastery does not offer an escape from the problems of life, so much as an alternative model for dealing with them. This model is based on an integrated balance of work and prayer, which should not be thought of as ends in themselves, but the necessary conditions for a life oriented towards what really matters. Indeed, these two activities, usually seen by us as being quite distinct, are to become for the monk one common endeavour.

The significance of work in the monastic context can be seen in a number of different ways. For example, in Benedict's era, the upper classes did not work; they had slaves to do it for them. By contrast, the monastery is a level playing field, where social status carries no weight, and rank is determined by date of entry into the community, 'regardless of age or distinction'.[62] Moreover, everyone is required to work, whoever they are or whoever they were before joining the monastery. One of the primary reasons for the emphasis on work is that Benedict does not want his monasteries to be a burden on society; they should be self-sufficient, containing within their walls 'all necessities, such as water, mill and garden'.[63] Paul and the apostles were self-supporting – so too should monks be, he says.[64] But work is not merely a practical requirement; it is also a spiritual necessity, which preserves the monk from the apathy and distractedness of acedia. Being occupied prevents us from indulging in fantasy worlds where everything is just as we want it to be. Properly understood, following a spiritual path is not about withdrawing from the world,

---

[62] RB 63.8.
[63] RB 66.6–7.
[64] RB 48.8.

but a different and arguably more challenging mode of being in the world.

Our usual attitude to work, however, is strictly utilitarian: simply a means to an end, which for many people is also a regrettable inconvenience. In our foundational myth – the allegory of the Fall – work becomes a mark of the unsatisfactoriness that characterizes the human condition: something we have to do, often grudgingly, because we have no choice. One way or another then, work is a fundamental component of our existence, yet so many people find the work they do unfulfilling, and instinctively feel there should be 'something more' to life, something that would make them feel more whole. This may be because we feel that our lives are somehow fragmented, split between the demands of our job and whatever it is we would rather be doing, whether that is something we have always dreamed of, or just the chance to spend more time with our friends and family. In a monastery we see how the practical and material dimensions of life – represented by work – can be integrated with the spiritual – what we truly value – to form a unified whole, a life lived 'in one piece'.

Work is considered by Benedict to be a necessary feature of the spiritual path, an essential responsibility to the community of which we are a part and also therefore to God. In the monastery, work is not regarded as just a way of making money, or something we have to do to pay the bills: we work because it is our duty to contribute to the common good. Benedict understood that while not everyone can be expected to do the same thing equally well, we all have different skills and abilities so everyone can, and must, do something for everyone. To serve others is to serve God; to serve God is to serve others by giving of the gifts we have been given. Monasticism is thus not about denying the worldly in order to cultivate the spiritual, but listening to all of life and responding appropriately. If we do the things we do in the spirit of humble service to God, and not for self-aggrandizement, then our work becomes the physical expression of our spiritual aspiration: we learn to see God in the washing up just as much as in the rituals of religion. The notion that the whole of life should be considered holy is clearly reflected in Benedict's instructions to the cellarer – the monastery's domestic manager – who is to regard 'all utensils and goods of the monastery as sacred vessels of the altar'.[65] This is how work becomes a form of 'prayer without ceasing'.

In the monastery, work and prayer are not treated as separate activities: not only does work become prayer, but prayer is the most important work a monk engages in. The monastic day is punctuated with regular periods of prayer, reminding the monk that simply being is sometimes more important than doing. Even important work must be interrupted to answer the call to prayer, although if a monk is away from the monastery – perhaps working in the fields – he should just pray where he is so as to be able to carry on with his work afterwards. Either way, prayer is understood as an integral part of everyday life, not something set apart from it. Thus Benedict urges the monk to consider nothing more important than this 'work of God'.[66] In an interesting conversation with a contemporary nun, it was suggested to me that the work of God – usually understood in terms of our duty to God expressed in prayer – might be more accurately understood

---

[65] RB 31.10.
[66] RB 43.1, 3.

as 'God's work'. In other words, the work God does *in us*. Our part is to make ourselves receptive to it, and that is what we call prayer: making ourselves open to the possibility of having God work in our lives.

In the *Rule* Benedict lists the enclosure of the monastery and stability in the community as two essential tools of the religious life.[67] These fundamental principles characterize most forms of monasticism to a greater or lesser extent; they are the outward expressions of the religious life that correspond to the equally essential interior principles of silence and humility. Together they represent the antithesis of the consumerism and individualism that seem to be the prevailing characteristics of contemporary culture. The question is, can these tools be of any use *to us*? Well, don't we all need, from time to time, to put things into perspective? Don't we all need a place we can go – even if it is only a mental place – that is set apart, enabling us to put a little distance between ourselves and everything that consumes us? And although we do not all live in monasteries and under a rule, we do all belong to communities of one sort or another, and we are all required to make choices and commitments in life – whether we like it or not – regarding work, marriage, family, friendships and so on. There is much we can learn from monks and nuns about how best to do these things, just as an amateur musician will be able to appreciate the skill of a professional, and learn something from listening to them play, even though they may never reach the same level of ability themselves.

---

[67] RB 4.78.

To be a monk is to be a stranger to the world. But at the same time, to devote one's life to the contemplation of God is not to be withdrawn and cut off from humanity. On the contrary, in the closeness of their relationship with God – in whom all creation has its being – the monk draws closer to other people. Similarly, by loving others he comes closer to God, for God – as Jesus said – is manifested in other people: 'For where two or three are gathered in my name, I am there among them.'[68] The claim that the life of prayer is a hidden ministry to the whole world should be perfectly coherent to anyone who can accept that life has a spiritual dimension. And yet monasticism is rarely understood, even within the church, in spite of the fact that being a monk or a nun is really no different from being any other kind of Christian – or human being, for that matter – because we are all programmed to seek what really matters. The only difference is that monks and nuns arguably take this a bit further than the rest of us.

---

[68] Matthew 18.20.

CHAPTER EIGHT
Seeing the Self as Other

Of the five participants in *The Monastery* TV series, I was probably the only one who had any idea of what I was letting myself in for, at least in terms of the monastic routine. I knew we would have to get up early, go to church a lot, and eat our meals in silence. If previous experience was anything to go by, I also knew I could expect to find it challenging, stimulating and fulfilling. What I could not anticipate, however, was the effect of sharing this experience with four strangers and a TV crew.

During the course of our stay it became apparent that our five-man micro-community, comprising people with very different attitudes to religion and widely divergent reasons for being there, provided us with first-hand experience of communal living deliberately intended to reflect the life of the monastery itself. The lesson we were to learn: that personal transformation only comes about through the rough and tumble of social interaction. Tensions inevitably emerged. I soon realized that both the dynamic of the group and the presence of the TV crew greatly intensified an experience that would probably have been intense enough already. As well as grappling with the challenges of the monastic discipline, and coping with each other, we were also constantly having to articulate for public consumption much that would normally have remained private. The positive side of this was that having to reflect on and verbalize my inner experiences for the benefit of the camera forced me to think about things that much more deeply. Because it is all on the record, we have been granted a rare and valuable opportunity to see ourselves as others might see us, as we really are – rather than as we think we are.

The one question people always ask (after 'how did you get on the programme?') is: 'did it change you?' It is usually obvious that they expect me to answer in the affirmative. It is less clear, however, whether that is because they think a monastery is a place where one might be likely to undergo some sort of personal transformation, or whether it is due to the fact that reality TV programmes so often feature the transformation of the participants (or their houses, gardens, lifestyle and so on). So while it may be a reasonable question to ask, it is also one that is not necessarily all that easy to answer; if only because there are effectively two monasteries to deal with here. On the one hand there was the real-life experience of going to live alongside a Benedictine community for six weeks; on the other, the media event of a popular TV series. In short, I have been through it all twice: once in reality, and then once again on reality TV. How much would my life have been affected had the experience not been televised, I wonder? Or how would I feel about it all now if the programme had been exploitative, or negatively received? It is impossible to leave the effect of the viewer out of the equation: the process of being observed contributed to the experience, even at the time, never mind afterwards.

There are two aspects of the observer effect to consider: the involvement of the filmmaker in setting things up, and the tendency for participants to show off in front of the camera. Regarding the former, we obviously would not have been there at all if it were not for the camera, and by extension therefore the viewer, who though physically absent, was nevertheless ever-present. It is inevitable that for practical reasons a certain amount of any documentary or factual programme will have to be staged; the manipulation of 'reality' is sometimes necessary simply in order to make filming possible in the first place. As it happens, in the case of *The Monastery*, intervention was fairly minimal – there were no games or tasks to perform – nevertheless, the distinction between fact and fiction in television is becoming increasingly porous. Reality TV draws heavily on narrative structures derived from soap opera, including the use of a single location, a central cast of characters, serial plot-lines, cliff-hangers at the end of episodes and the segmented interweaving of parallel storylines. All of these feature in *The Monastery*, together with other staples of the genre, such as the obligatory slanging match between argumentative participants, itself a standard motif in television drama.

We should not be surprised. Whether deliberately or unconsciously, a documentary filmmaker must necessarily create or select character storylines from the outset, according to their pre-conceived ideas about the story they intend to tell. This in turn affects not only editing once filming has been completed but also casting choices, decisions about what to film, the nature of the filmmaker's interaction with participants, the questions they ask and so on. Far from providing a neutral record of 'the facts', simply pointing a camera at someone is to intervene in the natural flow of life and impose a particular interpretation on a reality that in itself could be read in any number of different ways. Even if it is fair to say that what is seen in the programme is all true (well, almost), it is certainly not the whole truth, but a story told about our experiences by someone else, and from their point of view, not ours. Moreover, that story is bound to reflect the prevailing assumptions of the culture in which the storyteller is operating: in this case, those of the contemporary consumer society. Thus below the surface of *The Monastery* lies an implicit assumption that in order to 'sell' religion – with its awkwardly inexplicable reference to a divine transcendent reality – to a television audience, it must be repackaged in an easily digestible form, such as 'spiritual therapy' or a 'detox for the soul'. Ironically then, part of *The Monastery's* success can be explained as a function of the media's success in commodifying religious experience. By presenting religion as 'spirituality' – with all the attendant connotations of association without commitment – the programme subtly undermined its own subject matter. Regardless of its apparent claim to the contrary it did not challenge our consensual norms of individualism and consumerism, so much as confirm them.

As for the possibility that we might have been tempted to perform for the camera, either overtly or by being more guarded, the truth of the matter is that it is almost impossible to 'act naturally'. Even the phrase itself implies a contradiction. The problem is compounded by the fact that we expect people on television to play to the gallery. I can distinctly remember trying not to, but this too was a consequence of being observed, making the attempt to avoid acting an act in itself. Although I got used to the camera, and was perfectly relaxed about being filmed, I was still never entirely oblivious to its presence, nor completely indifferent to how I might come across. I don't think this marks me out as being especially self-conscious. Knowing that things said in private could one day be made public affected everyone's behaviour, and we were all aware of the difference when the crew were not around.

These observations allude to a deeper truth, however, which is that in normal everyday circumstances too, what we imagine to be the self is always and only a role: performed, not possessed. Having a camera pointed at us simply makes more obvious the fact that we are performing the role of our selves all the time. Indeed, it is no mere coincidence that the word personality comes from the Latin *persona*, the term for the mask that in classical drama an actor would wear to denote their character. And just as a character in a play only is that character if recognized as such by an audience, so our selfhood is validated by being seen by another. Who we are thus depends upon whom we are seen to be, and at the same time, our own self-conscious awareness of being seen. This may be why audiences instinctively feel they can get to 'really know' the participants in reality TV programmes, who often reveal something true about themselves in spite of their tendency to perform the self they wish others to see. Although *The Monastery* was undoubtedly conditioned by the notion of spirituality-as-therapy – not to mention the requirement of reality TV to be entertaining – nevertheless, the story of five men spending forty days in a Benedictine monastery revealed something real for and about the participants, which clearly communicated itself to the viewer.

Towards the end of our stay at Worth Abbey, the monks encouraged us to think about vocation – our role in life and our place in the world. "Vocation" said one of the brethren, "is all about discovering who we really are". To my mind, this was the whole point of the exercise: finding a way of being who we are meant to be in relation to what really matters. What I have come to realize about vocation is that it is not necessarily a question of what I *want* to do, but rather of doing what needs to be done; not a matter of my own choosing, but an honest response to the demand to be true to myself and true to God. It is to become an embodiment of that truthfulness and to be open to the possibility of undergoing radical transformation as a result. During my stay in the monastery I came to understand that the ascetic life of prayer and meditation – even, or perhaps especially, in its most introspective forms – is not so much about cultivating an intimate experience of one's self, but rather cultivating a relationship with something profoundly *other* than self. We only really come to know ourselves through others; not as we imagine we are, but by becoming aware of ourselves as others see us. Learning this simple but profound truth has, quite literally, brought me out of myself and into a fuller and more dynamic engagement with who I am and what I ought to be doing about it.

Monks and nuns, it seems to me, are people exploring the outer boundaries of inner space. From them I have discovered that the cultivation of 'self-knowledge' has nothing to do with indulging in a lot of self-obsessed navel-gazing. Quite the opposite, in fact. Only in relation to something other and beyond our selves can we know the deepest reality of what we are, the reality that some people call God. True self-knowledge therefore comes from seeing ourselves as others see us, and others as we see ourselves. Just as a bakery is a place where bread is made, so a monastery is a place dedicated to this particular task: the workshop in which the skills of self-awareness – seeing the self as and through other – are learned and cultivated. In that workshop, the person we think we are will be constantly undermined, as the masks we present to the world are worn away by the friction of rubbing up against other people. In one of the more curious stories in the Bible, Jacob spends the night wrestling with a 'stranger' (an angel or perhaps even God), and emerges from his struggle with the mysterious 'other' to become who he was really meant to be, as signified by the bestowal of a new name: 'You shall no longer be called Jacob, but Israel, for you have striven with God and with humans and have prevailed.'[69]

The cultivation of self-awareness requires that we engage with something other and more than ourselves, in a process of mutual give and take, which in turn depends upon an attitude of receptivity and openness. This is why the monastic tradition – following the teachings of Jesus in the Gospels – places so much emphasis on learning to see God in others, especially strangers and those in need. Benedict stresses that caring for the sick is of supreme importance, 'that they may truly be served as Christ',[70] and also that all who present themselves to the monastery as guests are to be received as if they were Christ himself.[71] Whether we are Christian or not, the meaning should be clear: what really matters is the other person. Being open to the stranger – who may have something important to teach us – and those who suffer and need our help, has the effect of dissolving the barriers that stand between us. By contrast, to put the self at the centre of our concerns – to be egocentric – isolates us from one another in a narcissistic world in which we behave as if others do not

---

[69] Genesis 32.28.
[70] RB 36.1.
[71] RB 53.1, 7.

really exist. Contrary to some of the more individualistic tendencies that seem to characterize the age in which we live, the monastic life shows how we can live for each other – not just ourselves – so that together we may become more than what we are on our own. To see what is other than us as being of ultimate concern is also to take responsibility for the consequences of our actions, and thus to make the world a better place for everyone. Hospitality can therefore be understood both in terms of receiving others into our personal space, and as taking care of the space we share. Until and unless we value others as much as we value ourselves, we can expect whatever problems we may have, both as individuals and as a society, to continue unresolved.

Thus when we talk about self-awareness we are actually talking about a new and heightened consciousness of that which is *other* than self. Knowledge requires an object, therefore it stands to reason that knowledge of the self requires the self to be seen objectively, as other than self, as others see us. Just as I can only see my face when it is objectified to me by being reflected in a mirror, so the self can only be known as it truly is when experienced through and as other: an other that transcends the boundary of our own subjectivity. This is illustrated in the desert tradition by a number of stories in which a monk apparently sees another who is then revealed to be themselves. For example, in a saying attributed to the desert nun Amma Theodora, there was once a monk who, on account of the number of temptations afflicting him, resolved to leave his place for somewhere less demanding. As he was putting on his sandals and getting ready to go, he caught sight of another monk doing the same. The second monk said to the first, 'Is it on my account that you are going away?

Because I go before you wherever you are going.'[72] This story not only reminds us that the things that plague us have an annoying tendency of following us wherever we go – we cannot run away from ourselves – but also that we only really come to self-understanding when we see ourselves as 'other'.

In practical terms, this means learning to see ourselves in the mirror of other people's behaviour towards us. Most of the time we go through life looking only at ourselves, or what we project of ourselves onto others. But if we were to be fully attentive to our interactions with other people, and our reactions to them – if we had self-awareness – we would see others as ourselves, and ourselves as others see us. According to Evagrius, 'A monk is one who esteems himself as one with all people because he ever believes he sees himself in each person.'[73] Similarly, it is a cliché – but nonetheless true – that the things we find most irritating in other people are very often the things we most have in common with them, for in others we see a reflection of ourselves.

The injunction 'know thyself', inscribed over the entrance to the temple at Delphi, has become a byword for the spiritual path in all times and all places. Not surprisingly, it is a central concern of Christian monasticism as well. When Poemen was asked how to become a monk, he replied: 'If you want to find rest in this life and the next, say at every moment, "Who am I?" and judge no one.'[74] However, this does not mean we simply assume a 'self', with which

---

[72] *Alphabetical Collection* Theodora 7.

[73] Evagrius, *On Prayer* 125.

[74] *Systematic Collection* Non Judgement 5.

we then strive to become better acquainted. Although we may talk about 'the self' in everyday conversation, closer examination reveals that it is not at all obvious what the word actually refers to. On the one hand, we have an irrefutable experience of being, which cries out for yet stubbornly resists explanation. On the other, our self is both the only thing about which we can justifiably claim to have exclusive knowledge, and at the same time the one thing we can never know; for just as we cannot see our own face, so we cannot find the self by seeking that which is doing the searching. If I follow Poemen's advice and ask 'who am I?' I discover that it is impossible to pin down a definitive answer. All I see is the various masks I present to myself and the world. If I try to see who is looking at that persona I find another mask, and another and another. Can the face behind the mask see itself, as it really is, in itself, when all the masks in which it is reflected and projected have been stripped away? Can I even be sure there's a 'face' behind the mask at all? I take Poemen's question to imply that in order – as he puts it – to 'find rest in this life', we have to let go of our rigid sense of who and what we think we are. But first we have to see the self for what it is: a case of mistaken identity.

In the Gospel, Jesus cautions us against laying up treasures on earth, 'where moth and rust consume', advising us instead to lay up treasures in heaven, for 'where your treasure is, there your heart will be also'.[75] In other words, our 'treasure' is what really matters, what we value most highly and identify with most closely – even to the point of being indistinguishable from it. If this is the case – that we

---

[75] Matthew 6.19–21.

are what we treasure – then what are the implications of investing our sense of self in our bodily identity, material wealth or worldly achievements? All these will pass away, consumed by moth and rust. We may find it relatively easy to see that we are not the things we own, but we will probably still identify with our memories, thoughts and feelings, regarding these as being somehow who and what we really are. Yet if anything, mental phenomena provide an even less sound basis for the notion of a 'true self'. This lack of a solid foundation is the reason why the mystics so often recall us to the fact of our mortality. 'Day by day remind yourself that you are going to die', says Benedict, exhorting his monks to treat what really matters as a matter of urgency.[76] By invoking the ultimate limit, the brute fact of non-being that threatens to render life meaningless, Benedict prompts us to be recollected to what makes life meaningful, to identify – as Jesus suggests – with that which does not pass away but is eternal: 'treasures in heaven, where neither moth nor rust consumes'.

The emphasis on self-denial in Christian monasticism also reminds us of the fact that the self is nothing in itself, but only what it is in relation to something profoundly other than self – whether neighbour or ultimately the ultimate reality that we call God. To consider something in isolation from its context, in itself so to speak, is to make the easy mistake of assuming an autonomous independent essence of things; it leads ultimately to solipsism. Identity is relational, not inherent. This is as true of people, as it is of institutions and things. In other words, an entity – of any description – is only what it is in

---

[76] RB 4.47.

relation to what it is not. At the heart of being is a mysterious emptiness: like the irreducible, self-evident 'I Am', it is not possible even to give it a name. There is also a sense in which we are empty because we are full of rubbish. Knowing the truth of this is humility, and humility – which is to say, learning what you are not – is the first step towards self-awareness, or learning who and what you are.

Unlike in the rest of life, worldly status – social class, intellectual or professional achievements, wealth and position – count for nothing in the monastery, where in contrast to the way of the world, 'we descend by exaltation and ascend by humility'.[77] In the *Rule* Benedict says: 'A man born free is not to be given higher rank than a slave who becomes a monk, except for some other good reason.'[78] He goes on to explain that the only valid measures of status in a monastery are good works and humility. Unfortunately, however, humility seems to be a rather unpopular word these days. Rejected as an essentially 'bad thing', humility is widely considered an unattractive characteristic – servile and pathological. Yet Benedict maintains that in the spiritual workshop of the monastery, where the hard shell of our constructed self is to be stripped away, layer by layer, true humility indicates not weakness, but great strength of character. The communal life, says Benedict, makes monks of 'the strong kind'.[79] This is because the essential requirement of a healthy community is that 'No one is to pursue what he judges better for himself, but instead, what he judges better for someone else.'[80] As we all know from our

---

[77] RB 7.7.
[78] RB 2.18.
[79] RB 1.12.
[80] RB 72.7.

own experience, if one person acts selfishly, putting their own interests before those of the group of which they are a part, then it causes immense disruption to everybody else. Living in a community – any community – is about putting the self at the service of the other. But this is not a one-way sacrifice. Putting others first does not entail submerging or denying the self: it leads not to the reduction of self, but – paradoxically – its fulfilment. Monasticism stresses the importance of mutual support. If I am present for others, then others are presumably present for my sake as well. To be truly open and present to the other, to live my life as if everything I thought and did was 'seen by God in heaven' and 'reported by angels at every hour',[81] as Benedict puts it, would be to take responsibility for all my thoughts and deeds: such accountability could not be anything but profoundly transformative.

By making us aware that we are not the centre of our own personal universe, that we are not what really matters, humility makes us present to others: it brings us into the humbling presence of a reality that transcends our limited individuality. Yet people still generally suppose that humility is all about denigrating oneself, or pretending to be worthless. In fact it is simply a matter of not showing off or making comparisons between ourselves and others. Monks are enjoined to 'judge no one', as Poemen said, and this is why they appear to be so calm and self-assured: they feel no need to compare themselves with others, because they see others as themselves. Numerous sayings from the desert fathers likewise focus on the theme of humility. Once, when a demon hit an old hermit on the jaw, he

---

[81] RB 7.13, Cf. 7.28, 19.1.

turned the other cheek. This display of humility burnt the demon like flames and he fled there and then.[82] To be humble is to remove the obstacles and close the gaps between ourselves and others: it is to see that we are not separate from one another – ultimately it is the basis of love. Humility and non-attachment therefore go hand in hand: they are both expressions of selflessness. And this is why humility is the most effective weapon against the obstructions of egotism that we personify as demons.

Jesus taught that we come to God – the highest good or 'what really matters' – through our neighbour, and in the monastic tradition we see this truth as a lived reality. Indeed it is one of the many paradoxes of monasticism that the path of interiority leads not to an encounter with the self – if that is understood in terms of an essentially private experience – but something radically *other* than the self. This is what it means to die to self; for self, ego, the tendency to judge or compare oneself with others, is the demon, so to speak, that comes between us and our fellow human beings. It is what prevents real contact, communication or communion from taking place, and keeps us trapped in the prison of our own mind and its delusions. We are not autonomous independent entities. On the contrary, who we are is defined in terms of that which is other than self; by our relationships: to the family, the work we do, our interests, the world, and so on. Our duty and purpose then, not necessarily as Christians, but simply as human beings, is to be a place where other people are able to encounter the divine; for God exists not only within, but also among us.

---

[82] *Systematic Collection* Humility 53.

CHAPTER NINE

Against the Grain

B enedict requires novices being received into the community to promise stability, conversion – or 'fidelity to the monastic life' – and obedience.[83] One of the first things we are likely to notice about these principles is that they are strikingly at odds with the values of contemporary society. This should not come as any surprise. Monasticism has always been profoundly countercultural, and monks deliberately cultivate the instinct, which deep down may be common to us all, of being strangers in the world. 'Your way of acting should be different from the world's way', says Benedict echoing St Paul, 'the love of Christ must come before all else'.[84] Flying in the face of convention, monks and nuns, now more than ever, bear fragile witness to a radical alternative to the prevailing consensus. Against restlessness and lack of commitment they emphasize stability, against complacency and conformity they advocate conversion of life, and against individualism and selfishness they stress obedience to one another.

In chapter one of the *Rule*, Benedict describes the four kinds of monks, and in so doing clearly indicates what he believes to be the positive attributes of, and negative hindrances to, the religious life.

---

[83] RB 58.17.
[84] RB 4.20–21.

The two types of which he approves, *cenobites* (who live in a monastic community), and *anchorites* (or hermits), are both characterized by the qualities of perseverance and rootedness; the former by virtue of the fact that they commit to a community and its rule, the latter because they have 'come through the test of living in a monastery for a long time'.[85] By contrast, fickle restlessness characterizes the 'disgraceful way of life' of the two kinds of monks he finds most detestable: the *sarabaites*, who 'do whatever strikes their fancy', embodying the pick and choose mentality so prevalent today, and the *gyrovagues*, the 'spirituality shoppers' of late antiquity, who drift around from monastery to monastery, 'slaves to their own wills and gross appetites'.[86] We may be used to thinking that travel broadens the mind, but in the monastic tradition, staying put is considered to be far more important. Amma Syncletica – an early female desert ascetic – believed that wandering from place to place would have a detrimental effect on a person, just as if a hen abandons her eggs they will not hatch.[87] The same attitude can also be seen in Benedict's reluctance to allow his monks to travel, albeit a restriction that might sound rather severe to those of us accustomed to frequent overseas holidays. In the *Rule* he writes that no-one may leave the enclosure without permission, nor speak about what they have seen outside when they return, because it is liable to have a disruptive effect on the rest of the community.[88] Indeed, so important is the promise of stability required of novices entering the monastery that

---

[85] RB 1.3.
[86] RB 1.8–11.
[87] *Alphabetical Collection* Syncletica 6.
[88] RB 67.5.

Benedict sees fit to mention it twice.[89] But stability is not only applicable to monks and nuns: Benedict maintains that stability – or sticking at it – is one of the necessary conditions for spiritual growth, and this applies to all of us.

The world today has much in common with the world in which Benedict lived: it is deeply unstable. Wars are being fought all around the globe, and even in peacetime many people live under the constant threat of terrorist attacks. An attitude of 'spend now, pay later' takes the waiting out of wanting, but also leads to the creation of a crippling debt culture that makes us all vulnerable to the vagaries of economic forces beyond our control. Perhaps even more alarming is the fact that the planet itself, thanks to our carelessness, is becoming increasingly unstable, as unpredictable climate change threatens to cause global environmental catastrophe. At the same time, rapid technological progress, which may be exciting for some, leaves others disoriented and confused, and requires us to upgrade continually in order to keep step with the pace of change. Indeed, consumption has become an end in itself: its purpose is not the satisfaction of our needs but their constant stimulation.

Even our identities are in flux – if not crisis. We are no longer souls but consumers, defined by where we shop and what we watch on television. By buying into brand labels, we acquire not only an image, but also a set of values to live by. Indeed for some people brand loyalty may provide the only semblance of community they are likely to experience – and even that is pretty shaky, as trends come and go with the changing seasons. All in all, life seems to have

---

[89] RB 58.9, 17.

become very fragmented: roles and expectations are blurred and ill-defined, leaving many people deeply troubled by a real anxiety about their place in society. Some respond by escaping into virtual worlds sustained by the entertainment industry and 'celebrity culture'; others by indulging in hedonistic excess to ward off their thinly-veiled despair. Meanwhile, all our familiar social structures are disintegrating around us: the notion of the 'typical' nuclear family seems like a nostalgic fairy-tale, and job security is for many a thing of the past.

There is also a psychological instability that can be identified in the common tendency to imagine that everything would be so much better if only things were 'just so'. This is a symptom of a problem very familiar to the monastic tradition – acedia – the restless boredom and idle fantasizing which gnaws insidiously at the monk, inducing him to give up the game. We experience it whenever we think that if only I had such-and-such, then I would be happy, or if only . . . if only anything. Whatever it might be, the likelihood is that we are fooling ourselves, and in denial about the reality of the here and now. Benedict was clearly all too familiar with the fickle nature of human beings, our tendency to give up when things get difficult. In the *Rule* he writes: 'Do not be daunted immediately by fear and run away from the road that leads to salvation.'[90] In other words, unless we persevere in a task we cannot expect a fruitful outcome, just as 'a tree cannot bear fruit if it is often transplanted'.[91] The truth of this is nowhere more vividly illustrated than in the story of

---

[90] RB Prologue 48.
[91] *Systematic Collection* Fortitude 36.

John the Dwarf, a desert monk whose master stuck a dead stick in the ground and ordered him to water it every day. This he did, though it would take him from dusk till dawn to fetch water from the nearest well. After three years, the stick turned green and sprouted.[92] By contrast, we allow ourselves to be put off by the slightest inconvenience, or distracted by what appear to be more attractive options. Too ready to give up, always seeking the quick fix, we tend to blame external circumstances for our frustration and unhappiness when, more often than not, the problem is as likely to be our own reluctance to take responsibility. But we are not just passive victims of forces beyond our control: we cause much of this instability ourselves, which suggests that it is born of a deep inner restlessness. We have become accustomed to a culture of unlimited choice and instant gratification, we demand constant stimulation and distraction, and are unwilling or afraid to be alone and silent.

For the monk, stability refers specifically to a commitment to remain in a particular monastery for life, but it should be clear by now that all of us – not just monks and nuns – could probably do with a bit of stability in our lives. Having stability implies engaging fully with the situation at hand, persevering in the face of obstacles and in spite of what might appear to be more appealing prospects. Stability is about being centred, remaining focused and un-distracted. In other words, it is to realize and accept that wherever we are, we are in the right place at the right time, doing whatever it is that needs to be done. It is important to note, however, that this is not the same as being fatalistic: the circumstances we find ourselves in

[92] *Alphabetical Collection* John the Dwarf 1.

may require us to contend against them. Nevertheless, in order to engage more effectively with any situation we have to accept that wherever we are, we are there to do a job. 'Sticking at it' is not, for Benedict, just a way of ensuring we all buckle down, accept our lot, and get on with things in order to maintain the status quo. It is not about stubbornly refusing to budge, or remaining static, but the determination to keep going. Whether we like it or not, some things cannot and do not happen instantly; they need time to grow and mature. We see this most clearly in terms of personal relationships. For example, getting to know someone properly takes time, and may involve periods of trial and difficulty that need to be worked out before a deeper level of trust and acceptance can be reached.

The second Benedictine principle, conversion – which refers to the turning around of one's life necessitated by entry into the cloister – might, at first glance, seem contradictory. It is almost as if Benedict is advocating stability on the one hand, while simultaneously demanding change on the other. We must understand, however, that the deliberate and purposive change of direction implied by conversion is very different from the aimless restlessness that would be the opposite of stability. In fact stability is the necessary correlate of conversion, precisely because conversion here means turning away from that restlessness so characteristic of 'normal' life – which often masks our inner purposelessness – towards the truth or value that is the point of everything. Conversion is therefore about transformation, but this transformation is not just a case of changing some superficial aspects of our behaviour, like going on a diet or giving up chocolate for Lent. It is something deeper and more radical than that. Conversion means becoming a different person, permanently, and turning towards a new life in which we strive to become more fully who we are really meant to be.

To understand this clearly, it may help to consider its opposite, which I would characterize as a kind of complacency: the absence of any awareness that there might be a problem that needs sorting out – presumably because we think everything is fine just as it is. Such complacency is based on an underlying assumption that this life (or world, for that matter), is all there is; and that satisfying the dictates of pride, sensuality and acquisitiveness is what really matters. The result is a tendency to just daydream through life, accepting it at face value, satisfied – like the Romans – with 'bread and circuses'. At the same time, we are for the most part unaware of our complacency – indeed we are quite seduced by it – so we resist real change by anchoring our identity to false notions of self; idols that we imagine to be durable and solid but which are actually ephemeral and transient. Why turn away from the gods of power, pleasure, and wealth in favour of a life of self-denial? Surely happiness lies in the pursuit or 'worship' of the former, while the latter would just be utterly miserable?

According to Benedict, the opposite is true. He urges us to consider that the way to true freedom and happiness involves turning away from the vain pursuit of material goals and selfish agendas, and putting God, or 'what really matters', at the centre of life. So how do we focus our restless desire on that alone in which we will find the eternal rest we truly seek? We are told that desire should not be repressed but sublimated; that the longing for worldly pleasures should be transformed into the desire for God. We are told that we should want this more than a drowning man wants air, and that if we truly understood the nature of suffering we would surely have no hesitation in renouncing the craving that causes it. Yet the reality is that we find it difficult to make the necessary change in orientation from worldly desire to spiritual desire, because the promised reward of spiritual discipline is not immediately apparent but has to be accepted on trust, whereas the satisfaction of worldly desires is instant. Especially these days. No wonder it can be so hard to sustain the hope for delayed gratification implied by the sacrifices required of the spiritual path.

Many religious traditions teach that to be truly free means to be free from the dictates of the ego, free from the incessant demands of our unquenchable desires, free from the bondage of greed, hatred and delusion, free to give rather than always and only ever wanting to take. 'This message of mine is for you, then', says Benedict, 'if you are ready to give up your own will, once and for all, and armed with the strong and noble weapons of obedience to do battle for the true King, Christ the Lord'.[93] To be conformed to the will of God is to be true to self; it is to know what really matters, what is of ultimate value, what one *really* wants. To be in union with what is, the way things are, is to answer the call of that deeper longing – manifested in the meantime as all our misplaced desires for the things of the world – which can only really be satisfied by, as it were, giving itself away. This is the freedom to be who and what you are really meant to be. It is not about what 'I want', but quite the opposite, for the desire underlying all our desires is the desire for peace, which ironically is a desire for the cessation of desire.

---

[93] RB Prologue 3.

And yet the notion that freedom means being able to indulge every whim and fancy remains stubbornly persistent. 'If it feels good, do it.' Never mind anybody else. By contrast, the monk 'loves not his own will nor takes pleasure in the satisfaction of his desires'.[94] Furthermore, in the monastery, 'no one may presume to give, receive or retain anything as his own [. . .] since monks may not have the free disposal even of their own bodies and wills'.[95] This probably sounds harsh – perhaps unacceptable – to modern ears, accustomed as we are to being able to have and to do whatever we want, *especially* with our bodies. We tend to believe that personal freedom – the freedom to express our own will – is the highest good, and we can be very intolerant of anything that seems to limit it. But what would a totally permissive society look like, with no limits whatsoever? It should not take us too long to realize that such a world might not be a very pleasant place in which to live. If everyone could literally do whatever they wanted, mayhem would inevitably ensue because that freedom would include the freedom to do unto others that which they might not want to have done to them. As we saw earlier, freedom is actually defined by what limits it. I have discovered that despite – or perhaps because of – the restrictions imposed by their vows of obedience and the enclosure of the monastery, monks and nuns are, ironically, a good deal more free than any of us, because they are free of the conditioning by which the rest of us are enslaved.

Benedict is, not surprisingly, keen on obedience. 'In the monastery', he says, 'no one is to follow his own heart's desire'.[96] Elsewhere

---

[94] RB 7.31.

[95] RB 33.2–4.

[96] RB 3.8.

in the *Rule* he encourages his monks to 'hate the urgings of self-will'.[97] At first glance, this sounds like exactly the sort of repressive authoritarianism that we might ordinarily take to be the exact opposite of freedom. All the more surprising then, that when we look at what Benedict actually understands obedience to mean, we discover that he claims obedience is the way to true freedom because it is ultimately equated with love. Freedom, according to Benedict, is not the kind of freedom we associate with gratifying our personal wishes: it is a freedom that comes from giving, not taking. In other words it is a freedom that results from being totally absorbed in, or given to, something other and perhaps greater than ourselves, like the freedom we experience when we lose ourselves in playing a musical instrument, for example. Here our limited egocentric self is subordinated to the discipline of the music, but being identified with something other and beyond, also transcends itself as a result.

According to Benedict, obedience is nothing to do with slavish adherence to rules and regulations, or being compelled to do things we don't want to do – that's the whole point – true obedience is an act of will, freely chosen, not grudgingly given. This highlights the subtle but important difference between power, which is imposed by force; and authority, which is earned or given. For Benedict, obedience willingly given is love; and love, under obedience, is freedom. Contrary to what we might ordinarily suppose to be the case, obedience requires us to lose nothing in order to gain everything; it is not the opposite of freedom, but the beginning of freedom. In the monastery, Benedict requires that obedience be shown not only to the

---

[97] RB 4.60.

Abbot, but also to one another, since 'it is by this way of obedience that we go to God'.[98] Obedience means listening attentively and responding appropriately, in order to give up all that comes between ourselves and others, and ultimately God. It is to open ourselves to the possibility of loving and of being loved.

Benedict describes his *Rule* as a little book 'for beginners'.[99] This is to say we are all pilgrims on the journey of life – there are no experts, we are all beginners – and nobody can ever learn anything without listening to others. In order to understand this fully, there are two things we need to realize. The first is that obedience really does literally mean 'listening' (from the Latin *audire*, to hear). The second, that what obstructs listening is what Benedict calls 'murmuring'.

The notion of murmuring originally derives from the biblical books of Exodus and Numbers, in which we repeatedly hear about the Israelites grumbling and complaining against God and against their leaders Moses and Aaron.[100] Consequently, God is always having to chastise them, saying things like: 'How long will this wicked generation grumble against me?' Modern English translations of the Bible often use the word 'grumbling' here, but the Bible Benedict knew – Jerome's Vulgate translation – used the word *murmuratio*, and this is the term we find in the *Rule*. 'Murmuring', with its sense of being only semi-audible (literally not *audire*, and thus not obedient) conveys better the insidious and poisonous habit that prevents an attentive attitude to life and to one another. In the monastic

---

[98] RB 71.1–2.
[99] RB 73.8.
[100] To give a few examples, Numbers 11.1; 13.31; 14.2, 27, 29, 36; 16.11, 41; 17.5.

tradition, murmuring becomes a very specific technical term, refer-ring to the incessant complaining and bickering, the all-pervasive negativity, that precludes listening, blocks communication, and stands in the way of our relationships – with the world, other people, God and ourselves. As we all know from personal experience, the result of poor communication is conflict.

Benedict explicitly denounces murmuring at several points in the *Rule*, for example where he says: 'If a disciple obeys grudgingly and murmurs, not only aloud but also in his heart, then even though he carries out the order, his action will not be accepted with favour by God, who sees that he is murmuring in his heart.'[101] As an aside, it is interesting to note that Benedict also disapproves of laughter, saying: 'We absolutely condemn in all places any vulgarity and gossip and talk leading to laughter.'[102] This may strike the modern reader as being rather harsh; we generally think that 'having a bit of a laugh' is a good thing. And so it is. Nevertheless, Benedict is making an important point here because – as with murmuring – when we laugh we are not being mindful. More importantly, laughter – especially the raucous laughter that Benedict is specifically referring to – invar-iably comes at someone else's expense.

Just to be clear, murmuring is not the same as making a legitimate complaint, for which there are, or at least should be, appropriate channels. It is rather the corrosive, bitter, and negative whispering that prevents listening and destroys all good feeling. It is gossiping, chitchat, backstabbing and snide remarks. And I am afraid we are all

---

[101] RB 5.17–19.
[102] RB 6.8.

at it, all the time – often without even being aware of it – both consciously when we are explicitly grumbling about things, blaming the world and each other for what are often enough our own faults, and subconsciously when we engage in the more subtle murmuring that is our almost constant internal commentary. Murmuring need not always be a direct disagreement; essentially it manifests as the habit of comparing others unfavourably with oneself, or mentally noting how things would be so much better if only they were done my way. 'Why did he do it like that? It's all wrong.' Or, 'It was so unreasonable of her to say such-and-such to me this morning.' The assumption being, of course, that we would never behave like that! In fact, I would be willing to bet that you are murmuring right now, even as you read this book – especially those bits where you disagree with me. And you have been having imaginary conversations with people you know, distractedly thinking about things you should be doing, or simply making plans for later. As I said, we all do this, all the time: it is what makes us 'absent minded'. But the most important thing we need to remember about murmuring is that it usually says a lot more about the one who is doing the murmuring than what they are supposedly murmuring about.

Unfortunately this kind of subtle murmuring is our default background state of mind. Most of the time we do not even realize we are doing it – let alone how poisonous and destructive it can be. We are, for the most part, so absorbed in our own egocentric concerns and caught up in our internal commentary – in short, murmuring – that we are not present to the reality of the here and now, the person standing before us, whoever they may be. To put it another way, we cannot possibly be listening if there is a voice in our heads that is already talking, diverting our energy and attention away from the present, preventing us from being present – to ourselves, to each other, and ultimately to the reality of God. A saying of Abba Poemen makes this point well: 'A man may seem to be silent, but if his heart is condemning others he is babbling ceaselessly. But there may be another who talks from morning till night and yet he is truly silent; that is, he says nothing that is not profitable.'[103]

More than anything else, murmuring reveals the activity of the demons, or obsessive thoughts and obstructions, so vividly described by Evagrius: thus to be aware of our mental chatter is to exercise the discretion he advocates. Similarly, Benedict urges his monks to cultivate mindful awareness, saying: 'Hour by hour keep careful watch over all you do, aware that God's gaze is upon you, wherever you may be.'[104] Elsewhere he talks about what I would identify as the practice of mindfulness in the following terms: 'While he guards himself at every moment from sins and vices of thought or tongue, of hand or foot, of self-will or bodily desire, let him recall that he is always seen by God.'[105] This is what it means to be self-aware: aware of oneself as an object of another's awareness. And this is why the spiritual life is about learning to 'be silent and listen'.[106] 'Listen' is the first word of the *Rule*, 'Listen with the ear of your heart',[107] says Benedict. This is the beginning and end of his teaching.

---

[103] *Alphabetical Collection* Poemen 27.
[104] RB 4.48–50.
[105] RB 7.12.
[106] RB 6.6.
[107] RB Prologue 1.

CHAPTER TEN

Being Still

About half-way through our stay at Worth Abbey we were taken to visit Parkminster, the Carthusian monastery – or Charterhouse – near Horsham in Sussex. I was quite simply awestruck. If you want to see what the monastic life looks like when pushed to its absolute limits, or where the path of renunciation leads when taken to its logical conclusion, then look no further than the unmarked rough wooden crosses of a Carthusian cemetery. The order has a well-deserved reputation for austerity. Founded by St Bruno in 1084, the Carthusians are famous for never having been reformed. Apparently they have never needed it, and it is not hard to see why. Parkminster is not like other monasteries – certainly not other monasteries in the modern world. There's none of that 'modern world' stuff here: these guys are doing things the old-fashioned way. Nonetheless, the monks' cells, no doubt forbidding to some – they contain nothing but a bed, desk and prayer stall – had, to my eyes, a simple but devastating beauty that shone from the bare walls and burned itself into my mind.

It was only a short visit, just enough time for a quick look round, but in that brief encounter Dom Cyril, the novice-master, said something about prayer that really made sense to me. He was explaining that when novices joined the monastery they would start out with all sorts of ideas about God. After a while, these initial concepts would be gradually broken down and replaced by another understanding of God: more refined perhaps, but – inevitably – still a construct. In due course, this too would have to be deconstructed and abandoned. The same process would be repeated again and again until finally they would come to a state of pure awareness in which the naked reality of God is apprehended as he is in himself, free of our projections. I was immediately reminded of the sort of meditation practices I was familiar with from my experiences of Eastern religions. As if to confirm this intuition, Dom Cyril proceeded to tell us about a Zen Buddhist master who once came to stay with them in order to learn something about the Carthusian practice of prayer.

"In spite of the silence", said Dom Cyril, "We found we had a great deal in common; we could understand each other in the silence". Later, when I came across the works of Evagrius, I realized how closely the Carthusians have modelled themselves on the monks of the desert. In his treatise on prayer, Evagrius writes: 'When you pray do not form images of the divine within yourself, nor allow your mind to be impressed with any form, but approach the Immaterial immaterially and you will come to understanding.'[108]

For many years, I considered prayer to be little more than the mindless repetition of meaningless words during boring and irrelevant church services. At best, it was talking to yourself; at worst, superstitious mumbo-jumbo that vainly attempted to propitiate supernatural entities that in all likelihood did not even exist. The problem, of course, is that there is something about this caricature that rings true, which would be one explanation for the widespread

---

[108] Evagrius, *On Prayer* 66.

decline of what many people refer to as 'organized religion'. But that is only part of the story. Although we are not much interested in going to church, 'spirituality' – we are told – is all the rage. We may not see the point of prayer, but we cannot get enough of meditation. Underlying this state of affairs seems to be a belief that simply by using 'spiritual technology', we can achieve inner peace, self-knowledge and a calm, stress-free life – not to mention increased energy, concentration and productivity. Indeed some lifestyle gurus even promise the fulfilment of our material aspirations as well. Seen in this light, spirituality is reduced to little more than a set of positive-thinking strategies to help enhance our career prospects, or perhaps an exotic form of relaxation therapy. Ironically, there is a whiff of the old magical understanding of religion about this: it is using God to serve our own ends, rather than allowing ourselves to be really changed. For it to be truly transformative a spiritual practice requires us to engage with – and be accountable to – something other and more than our own self. This is most obviously the case with regard to the intentions expressed when we pray for others, but it also applies to the more interior and non-verbal forms of prayer as well.

Evagrius maintains that the mind is 'naturally constituted for prayer'.[109] He also says that 'prayer prepares the mind to exercise the activity that is proper to it'.[110] These statements would seem to suggest that prayer is our natural condition – a state of just quietly being. Thus, prayer is not about achieving goals; still less about having 'spiritual experiences', which in any case would be considered by

---

[109] Evagrius, *Praktikos* 49.
[110] Evagrius, *On Prayer* 83.

most traditions to be a distracting and deceptive product of emotion-alism. To be in harmony with 'what is' is simply to be; not something we do for the sake of the results and benefits that will accrue to us, great though they may be, but for its own sake, as a manifestation of love and therefore as an end in itself. Prayer, for Evagrius, is 'a com-munion of the mind with God'.[111] To put it another way, it is an abiding in that in which we truly are, in which 'we live and move and have our being'.[112]

Contemplative spirituality is about the fullness of being human. This is not necessarily to say that there is something 'out there' called 'the spiritual' without which our lives are incomplete, but rather that the fullness of being human is, by definition, what we use the lan-guage of spirituality to describe. That fullness involves the cultivation of self-awareness: being present to who and what and where and how we are, which in turn is likely to require a revolutionary conversion of life. I am more than happy to accept that there are many different ways in which this fullness can be attained, but I cannot help think-ing there is also a subtle but significant difference between what we might call techniques for 'self-improvement', and the cultivation of a deeper relationship with God. Or Truth, or Reality – if you prefer those words. This is not to say that matters of technique are not important, but that technique should not be our principal concern. Just as the act of opening a window does not in itself cause the cool refreshing breeze to blow in, so our practice – the skill we cultivate – is simply a means that enables or allows something to happen,

---

[111] Evagrius, *On Prayer* 3.
[112] Acts 17.28.

something over which we ultimately have no control. The most we can do is lay the groundwork, make ourselves open to a possibility, the possibility of what Christians would call grace. So it is less about technique than attitude; an attitude of openness and humility.

When people ask me about prayer or how to meditate, I usually reply: 'Just sit quietly and think of God.' But each part of this statement needs unpacking. First, sitting. As many people will be aware, in some traditions of Indian spirituality there is a particular emphasis on posture: after all, yoga is one of the most familiar brands in the contemporary spiritual marketplace. Those who practise it often lament what they regard as the neglect of the body in western spiritual traditions. Some may even go so far as to accuse Christianity of seeing the body as a positive *hindrance* to spiritual practice, but I think this view is mistaken. Christianity is not, on the whole, a world-denying religion. Christians believe that God created the world and deemed it to be good, that he made himself known to us in the human form of Jesus, that the church is the body of Christ (with whose body the faithful commune in the Eucharist), and that their own bodies will be resurrected after death. Therefore, the body is not like some piece of inconvenient baggage, or a set of worn-out clothes to be discarded at the end of our lives, but the outward form of the soul, and thus a profound expression of who and what we are.

Few people seem to be aware that Christian monks also attach a subtle but significant importance to matters of posture, especially when engaged in the corporate prayer of the divine office. In the *Rule*, Benedict says: 'Let us consider, then, how we ought to behave in the presence of God and his angels, and let us stand to sing the psalms in such a way that our minds are in harmony with our voices.'[113] This general principle will often be elaborated in the detailed regulations governing a monastic community, and might include specific instructions for the bodily attitude and conduct of novices. One monk of my acquaintance, a sprightly man in his eighties, always impressed me with his fine deportment, and I believe it is no coincidence that he had an aura of goodness to match. If it is true that our body language can sometimes say more than the actual words we utter, then it follows that the posture we adopt when we pray or meditate may say something significant about our relationship to what we are doing. For example, does it make a difference if we kneel, which conveys an attitude of supplication and reverence, or sit cross-legged, a posture suggesting self-containment? We may, for example, associate Christianity with the former and Buddhism with the latter, yet the fact is that when Buddhist monks chant the sutras, they do so kneeling. Indeed, Buddhists are very particular about matters of bodily demeanour. When visiting temples it is highly inappropriate to sit with your feet pointing towards the Buddha image, because in many Asian cultures the feet are regarded as the lowest part of the body, not only literally but also in terms of ritual purity. So I think it is important to give some consideration to our posture. Can we really pray properly when lounging in an armchair? Or lying in bed, for that matter? As a bare minimum I would recommend at least sitting with the back straight and unsupported, remaining still, in a posture that is relaxed and comfortable but also firm and steady.

---

[113] RB 19.6–7.

The claim made by practitioners of yoga that stillness of body leads to stillness of mind is not the exclusive preserve of Indian traditions: the desert fathers maintained that simply sitting still, preferably on or close to the ground, would greatly aid their attempts to keep the mind focused and thus resist the distracting chatter of demons. To sit still is to be present, and fully attentive to what is. How often do we really give our undivided attention to the things we do, or the people we are with? To be present is to accept what is as it is, and ourselves as we are, without wishing things were otherwise, or imagining that if only they were, then everything would be so much better. It is to be able to pick up a pebble and see that it is perfect – just as it is – neither too big nor too small. Paradoxically, being present requires a certain amount of distance. We need to be a little detached from the influence of passing moods, undisturbed by the many fluctuations we may experience in our feelings, so that we might be more present to what is actually going on, right there in front of us.

Being present might sound straightforward, but it is one of those things that is easier said than done. If it is hard enough to sit still, keeping the mind still is almost impossible. We are accustomed to such an extremely high level of stimulation in life that we probably do not even realize how distracted we are most of the time. The first time we meditate, we may even be distracted by the novelty of what we are doing: just trying to sit still and do nothing will probably feel rather peculiar to begin with, and it may be a while before we are comfortable with it. Alternatively, we might experience a run of 'beginner's luck', but this too can be distracting. As we settle down and turn our attention inwards, we will become aware that the mind consists not of ordered processes over which we preside like the conductor of an orchestra, but an unending succession of random thoughts and images. We will notice, perhaps for the first time, how we are caught up in an internal monologue, swept along by a river of words, and anything but present to the here and now. So before we can even begin to consider 'pure prayer', we need to see how scattered we really are, and therefore what it might be like for the mind to be still. Having achieved a degree of physical stillness, we need to draw the mind back from its aimless wanderings by trying to keep our attention focused on a single object, such as the breath, an icon, prayer word or mantra.

Any of these objects can be useful, but I wish to focus specifically on the breath. This is no arbitrary choice. Concentration and steady breathing go naturally together: we are all familiar with the experience of taking a deep breath to calm ourselves down. One of the significant things about breathing is that although it is an automatic physiological process, it is also one that we can control to some extent – unlike our heartbeat or the workings of our kidneys, for example. Thus, we can make our breathing fast or slow, shallow or deep; we can even hold our breath for short periods and stop breathing altogether. This means that the breath can be seen as a link between body and mind, a bridge we can use in order to cross from a state of agitation and distraction to calm awareness of the here and now. None of which is to say that we should try and breathe in some special way when we meditate. On the contrary, our breathing should be relaxed and natural. Rather, the point is that if we breathe in a calm, gentle manner, it will have an immediate and corresponding effect on our mind. Moreover, because the breath connects the

spiritual and material dimensions of our being, it is often imbued with potent symbolism. In the Bible we hear how when God created Adam and Eve, he breathed the breath of life into them, and from this we get our notion of a soul or spirit. God's breath gave life, making the breath a direct link between creature and creator, us and God. Our breath is one of our vital signs, indicating that we are alive. It is also what we have in common with that which is the source of all that is. Perhaps through it, therefore, we can re-connect with God.

If we were able to achieve perfect concentration, we would be fully aware of everything we do, all the time, to the point of being aware of every breath we take. Learning to concentrate is thus essential to the cultivation of awareness, but at the same time we should beware lest our efforts become a further source of distraction. We practise concentration in order to see just how restless and distracted the mind really is. Having seen it, we must learn to let go of our sense of personal involvement in that mental activity. This is why prayer, like listening (which is really what prayer is all about), is a state in which we need to be both relaxed and alert at the same time. If you can imagine being half asleep and dreaming while simultaneously being fully conscious and wide awake, watching your dreams without identifying with the person in them, then you have some idea of the kind of twilight zone I am talking about – neither day nor night – when the world takes on a different hue. This calls for a delicate balancing act. On the one hand, if we try too hard, we are imposing our will, the 'I' gets in the way and we will not reach the state of pure prayer, which Evagrius says will only arise when we are making no effort. On the other hand, a degree of conscious intention is necessary in order to keep our attention poised so that it does not wander away from the here and now and drift aimlessly in memory and fantasy.

People sometimes think that meditation is all about trying to stop the mind from thinking. One only need practise for a short time to realize that this is impossible, as the following story from the desert tradition so vividly illustrates. A monk comes to Abba Poemen and complains that he cannot do anything to stop the thoughts that come into his mind. Poemen tells the monk to go outside, and open his lungs without breathing. When the monk admits that he is unable to do this, Poemen says: 'Just as you can't stop air coming into your lungs, so you can't stop thoughts coming into your mind. Your part is to resist them.'[114] As well as emphasizing once more the link between breath and mind, the truth this story highlights is that thoughts come and go, largely unbidden, whether we like it or not. When we are consciously thinking about something, the mind seems orderly and focused. But if we manage to disengage the thinker, the mind does not just stop thinking: it idles in neutral, becoming a kaleidoscopic flux of random, churning images. We cannot stop this dream-like stream of consciousness, because that is just the mind being what the mind is. Moreover, to try to control or suppress it reinforces the ego, which would be counter-productive. What we can do is simply remain still, quietly observing the thoughts as they arise and then gently letting them go, without getting personally involved, without slipping into the starring role of our mental movie. Again this requires us to be both alert and relaxed: letting go requires a conscious effort. We may, for example, do it by labelling each

---

[114] *Systematic Collection* Discretion 55.

thought as we become aware of it, and then dropping it back into the void from which it came. This is where our ability to concentrate comes into play. To label and let go of each thought as it arises, without being carried away by it is no mean feat: it will prove almost impossible to maintain such a state of awareness for more than a few moments at a time. But that's all right. When Antony was distracted by restless thoughts, he saw a vision of a man like himself sitting at his work, getting up to pray, sitting down to work again, getting up to pray . . . 'Do this and you will be saved', the angel said to him.[115] Like Antony, we just have to keep at it.

As with any labelling process, it will help to have some way of classifying our thoughts. We looked earlier at one such scheme: that of the eight demons described by Evagrius. I wish now to propose something much simpler. Evagrius noted that thoughts consist of simple mental data, which we receive in the form of sense impressions. This data is then combined and compounded to produce complex ideas and feelings – in much the same way that words, though meaningless in themselves, can be arranged in an infinite number of ways to produce sentences and paragraphs that convey meaningful information. Thus the thoughts and feelings we have – and identify with as being I, me or mine – can be reduced to combinations and permutations of basic sensory information. If we sit quietly and observe the manipulation of this mental data, we will notice that every thought can be classified under one of two basic headings: memory or fantasy. That is to say, all our mental activity consists either of re-living the past or speculating about the future.

---

[115] *Alphabetical Collection* Antony 1.

Since neither memory nor fantasy presently exist, if we are caught up in our thoughts then we cannot be in the here and now, we cannot be present to God, the world, each other, or even ourselves. Prayer is the practice of letting go of all that stands between us and God; letting go of the 'me' that is most obviously manifested as the ceaseless chatter – or murmuring – of our inner voice.

If meditation was just about relaxation it would not be transformative, merely a pleasant rest. In fact, it is hard work – as the desert fathers would have been the first to point out. John the Dwarf is supposed to have told another hermit that his heart was at peace, 'with no war between flesh and spirit'. The hermit replied: 'Go and ask the Lord to stir up a new war in you. Fighting is good for the soul.'[116] The need to persevere in the face of adversity is repeatedly emphasized in monastic literature; spiritual life demands a certain amount of effort on our part, and we are likely to encounter obstructions from the outset. As well as contending against the demons of their obsessive thoughts, monks often had to prove their commitment to the life in other ways as well. Benedict stipulates that newcomers should not be given 'an easy entry',[117] and many sayings from the desert tradition tell of visitors being ignored until able to demonstrate the sincerity of their desire to be received.

Like any other discipline, it takes time to acquire proficiency in prayer, and effort to sustain it. But if we persevere, we may in due course cultivate sufficient mindfulness to avoid being distracted and losing our focus, at least for a few seconds. Thoughts will not cease as

---

[116] *Systematic Collection* Fortitude 8.
[117] RB 58.1.

long as there is breath in the body, but their constant flow might slow down a little, and if it does we may be able to discern a gap opening up between them. Like the desert itself, stretching as far as the eye can see, this inner space is truly silent, truly empty. In this gap, free from all the noise and clutter with which we normally fill our minds, it is possible to become aware of the still centre behind the surface activity of our conscious mind. We may even stop breathing for a few seconds, without being aware of having done so. Forgetting for a moment the aching in our knees, or indeed that we are a body at all, we may experience ourselves as unlimited consciousness: just being; pure stillness. Letting go of our identification with the body, thoughts, sensations, memories and feelings, says Evagrius, 'being filled with both reverence and joy, then consider yourself to be near the frontiers of prayer'.[118] In this empty space at the heart of being we may become open to the possibility of an encounter with what is – present to the presence of God.

Pure prayer is characterized by Evagrius as being when the mind becomes 'immaterial and free from all things' and acquires 'perfect detachment from the senses'.[119] As we saw earlier, this state depends on cultivating *apatheia*, which is the necessary precondition for prayer, and the outcome of the mindfulness he describes as the discernment of thoughts. Hence, 'You cannot practise pure prayer while entangled in material things and agitated by continuous concerns, for prayer is the laying aside of mental representations.'[120] This brings

---

[118] Evagrius, *On Prayer* 61.

[119] Evagrius, *On Prayer* 119–20.

[120] Evagrius, *On Prayer* 70.

us back to where we began this chapter, with the notion of prayer as a process of breaking down our concepts of God. 'Prayer', says Evagrius, 'is a state of the mind destructive of every earthly representation'.[121] Needless to say, Evagrius attributes our mental constructs of God to the work of demons, particularly the demon of vanity. It is because of vanity, he says, that the mind tries to confine the divine 'in forms and figures'.[122] It is vanity to think that one has understood what is beyond human understanding. Our concepts of God are thus merely projections of ourselves onto the blank canvas of truth, or attempts to process the chaos that is reality. God, in himself, is nothing that we can think.

"But if all our ideas of God are constructs, how do we know that the 'other' we think we encounter in contemplation is not just another deluded projection of self?" I asked Dom Cyril.

"We don't!" he replied with a chuckle, "At least not at the time. If we are conscious during prayer that we are praying, we are not really praying the true 'prayer of the heart'. It is only afterwards that we can know whether or not we were really there." Once again, Dom Cyril was echoing the desert tradition. Evagrius states that 'Just as when we are asleep we do not know that we sleep, so neither when we are contemplating do we know that we have passed into contemplation.'[123] Cassian makes the same point, quoting Antony as having said that it is not perfect prayer if 'the monk understands himself or

---

[121] Evagrius, *Reflections* 26.

[122] Evagrius, *On Prayer* 116.

[123] Columba Stewart, *Cassian the Monk* (Oxford: Oxford University Press, 1998), p. 114.

what he is praying'.[124] In the state of 'pure prayer' we are not aware of ourselves as separate, individual beings, for pure prayer is an experience of oneness with God, in which our own selves are laid aside and we realize the divine that is all that is. What we call 'spiritual practice' then, is the process of removing all the noise that fills the mind and obstructs this awareness.

"You have to lose yourself in order to find yourself", explained Dom Cyril, echoing the well-known Gospel narrative, "but not by making the self the object of your search; rather by letting yourself be open to the possibility of being found by God". In this sense there is no need to seek God, for God is the ground of our being, the deepest reality of what we are, and closer to us, as the Qu'ran so vividly expresses it, than our own jugular vein. This is why Evagrius says: 'You want to know God? First know yourself.'[125] To know others – or for that matter the ultimate other that is God – we must first know ourselves, but we only come to know ourselves by knowing others. Paradoxically, the result of going deeper into the self is that we draw closer to others; for the deepest reality of what we are is the ground of being we all share.

After that first visit to Parkminster I sat in the church at Worth Abbey, alone and in stunned silence, for several hours. Most of the rest of the day was spent trying, not always successfully, to hold back the tears. At the time I didn't really understand what made me want to cry. I knew I had caught a glimpse of what really matters, and at the same time I knew that it would remain forever beyond my reach.

---

[124] Ramsey, *Conferences*, p. 349.
[125] Evagrius, *Maxims* 2.2.

Only later did I make the connection with the story of the rich young man, who – upon being told what he must do to attain eternal life – turned his back in sadness and walked away, knowing that he could not give up his world. I thought again about the day, when sitting on the banks of the Ganges at Rishikesh, I had committed myself to the spiritual life. Where had it led me? I felt lost. And at the same time inspired. On our first meeting, Dom Cyril struck me as someone who really knew what he was talking about. He had been there and done it. And let's face it, there are not many of whom one can say that.

I stayed in touch and, the following year, returned to do a one-month retreat in a Carthusian cell. I was very excited by the prospect, and a little apprehensive too. I knew it would be challenging, but also hoped it would be fulfilling. In a letter confirming the dates, I was instructed to bring a good pair of walking shoes, and no unfinished business. Slightly tongue in cheek, I wrote back saying I would make sure not to bring any unfinished business, but that if it was okay I might bring some unread books. The reply was brief but to the point: "No problem about bringing some books. We can discuss their use on your arrival." I decided to leave the books at home with the unfinished business.

CHAPTER ELEVEN

Silence

"The first forty-eight hours are the worst", said a Benedictine monk of my acquaintance when I told him I was going to be spending a month at Parkminster. "But if you can get through that you'll be fine!" he added cheerfully. Helpful advice, no doubt, but still – not exactly reassuring. Nowadays, few religious communities live up to the typical monastic clichés of austerity and self-denial; indeed some are really quite comfortable. The Carthusians, by contrast, reinforce all the popular stereotypes. And then some. The cool, vast, empty cloister – which never seems to warm up, even in summer – is home to a community whose way of life has remained largely unchanged for hundreds of years. Although it was only built in the late nineteenth century, the sight of hooded monks silently making their way to church in the middle of the night conveys the unmistakeable impression that Parkminster is in every respect a living medieval monastery.

During the month I spent there, I never quite managed to shake the feeling that I had stepped back in time, nor did I ever get used to the fact that there really are people still doing this today, in Britain, and through their own choice. Their cloistered life, by any measure of what most people would consider normal, is completely unnatural. The Carthusians see themselves as heirs to the desert fathers, and they deliberately strive to re-create the ethos of early Egyptian monasticism by being a community of hermits. Are they the ultimate escapists, or the most deeply engaged with the reality of being human? At times I couldn't help thinking they had to be completely mad. Yet at other times it was clear that they were not only more sane, but also more free than any of us.

Well, the first forty-eight hours were pretty tough. And I say that as someone who really enjoys being in these places. I have stayed in monasteries where I have had nothing but a hard pallet to sleep on. I have happily risen at four o'clock every morning to spend two hours in silent prayer before dawn. I have shared a cell with rats, allowed mosquitoes to bite me while I meditated, and sat cross-legged under a tree with my back to a cobra's lair. Monasteries, in short, are my thing, and I had been eagerly looking forward to my stay at Parkminster for months. The place is legendary: monks of other orders speak about it in hushed tones. "That's a *real* monastery", they say with a mixture of admiration and horror.

It's not easy to get into Parkminster, and of the few who do, most can't wait to get out again. Those who manage to stick it out, however, seldom leave unaffected. Like a mountaineer who dreams of Everest, I yearned to taste their way of life for myself, and fully expected to be bowled over, if not transported to higher planes. Shortly after my arrival – in fact, almost as soon as I found myself alone in my cell – it slowly dawned on me: this was not going to be much fun. The isolation is almost total. Not only is there no contact with the outside world – no newspapers, radio, TV or internet – but very few concessions to the basic comforts of modern life that the rest of us take for granted. There is electricity – it was put in during the 1970s – but no hot water or central heating. Food is simple, furnishing minimal and certainly not soft. There are no carpets, curtains, or comfy armchairs. My iron bedstead was tiny, the lumpy horsehair mattress and coarse blankets, covered in patches, looked as if they could have been as old as the monastery itself. Having said that, my cell was not completely devoid of creature comforts. A little stack of logs lay neatly piled beside the wood-burning stove, and – appropriately enough – a copy of the *Sayings of the Desert Fathers* was waiting for me on the desk.

For the first few days, however, I was miserable. Disappointed with myself for not enjoying it, and stunned by what seemed to be a joyless and implacable regime, it felt like an endurance test. It was not only the solitude and the silence that got to me, but the feeling of being totally cut off from the world. I am not averse to spending time on my own at home. I do not feel the need for constant company and distraction; I am quite content to just get on with doing my own thing. But in such circumstances, and even if I don't see anybody all day, I can still make phone calls, listen to music, read the papers or go for a walk. Not here.

But I persevered.

Many do not apparently, and Carthusians delight in stories of people who come to them with all sorts of romantic notions of being a monk, imagining they want nothing more than to spend the rest of their days in silent contemplation, only to beg to be let out again as soon as possible. I may have been tempted to run away myself on a couple of occasions, especially to begin with, but I was determined to do my time and I am glad that I did. As one of the brethren later pointed out, there is a big difference between seeking an experience, and seeking that which it is an experience of. After a period of acclimatization – probably about a week – I gradually began to appreciate life in the artificial desert of the Charterhouse, even though the severity of the discipline never really became any easier to endure. Clearly it would take a lot longer than a month to get used to rising at midnight to spend three hours in church. Not to mention the lack of coffee, having no choice about what I ate (and to be honest, monastic catering can leave a little to be desired), nothing but bread and water on Fridays, and cold showers. But far harder than all these physical privations was the mental discipline of just being present. This was what Dom Cyril would always emphasize when he dropped by every few days to check up on me.

"Just be here", he would say, echoing Abba Moses, the desert father who famously said: 'Go, sit in your cell, and your cell will teach you everything.'[126] And for the first week or so he would always ask, "Are you here yet?" It took me a little while to understand what he really meant. Completely removed from all the business of everyday life, I became very aware that most of my time was being spent elsewhere: thinking about all the things I could or should be doing, the people I might have been seeing, what I would do when I got out, and so on. Indeed, much of this idle daydreaming was taken up with making plans for the future, surely the most pointless of enterprises and a clear sign of a distracted and unfocused mind. But slowly I began to notice how the silence, discipline, and ironically even the enclosure itself – which seemed so restrictive at first – actually allowed for the opening up of a new interior space, free and still, that I am not normally aware of.

---

[126] *Alphabetical Collection* Moses 6.

More often than not, however, we seem to find silence slightly disturbing: when we find ourselves in a quiet place, we immediately want to fill it with noise. Indeed, we even talk about an 'awkward silence' that descends on a social gathering when people run out of things to say to each other. But why should silence be awkward? Why do we feel it necessary to avoid silence at all costs, even if it means talking rubbish to keep silence at bay? Why do we find it so difficult to cope with being alone or silent? It is as if we think that silence is somehow unnatural, as if nature 'abhors a vacuum'. Sometimes we find it hard to break a silence, even to the extent that we might feel uncomfortable or embarrassed as we desperately try to think of something to say. But to talk about breaking a silence implies that silence is something whole. According to the biblical creation story, in the beginning there was silence, the formless void, the chaos out of which creation emerges, the whole from which the part is differentiated. God breaks that awkward silence with his creative word and in so doing brings the world into being. If our world is a world constructed by language, then to know silence is to know reality as it really is.

For all the emphasis on silence and solitude, however, the Carthusians are still a community, and the communal aspect of their life is vitally important. As well as gathering in church three times a day, they also go for a long walk through the local countryside on Monday afternoons. This is the only time they are able to talk to one another, and apart from chopping logs for the winter, or gardening, it may also be the only physical exercise they get. During my first week I was not allowed to join the walk – Dom Cyril wanted me to settle in properly first – so by the time I did get to go, I had already been there nine days. Nine days without meeting any of the other people that I nevertheless knew were there, sharing the silence around me. Nine days without being able to put names to any of the faces of the shadowy figures with whom I spent four and a half hours in church every day. And yet at the same time, because everyone always sits in the same place, during those nine days I became very familiar with the monks on either side of me – just from their physical presence – even though I didn't know the most basic thing about them: their names.

By the second week, I was a little apprehensive about going on the walk. What would we talk about? Would it feel awkward breaking the silence? What if no one said anything? We paired up and set off. After so many days with no conversation at all, I suddenly became acutely aware of the extent to which we take our normal social interaction for granted, and that we must fail to really hear one another as a result – not to mention how banal and disposable much of our everyday chatter is. Walking in twos, and changing partners every half hour, these brief but intense encounters allowed no time for commerce in mundane pleasantries: after the most cursory of introductions we just plunged straight in. I was amazed by the amount of information that could be exchanged in such a short period of time. In a single afternoon I discussed everything from the Spanish civil war to popular Hollywood movies. I also heard half a dozen fascinating life-stories.

A monk is one who withdraws to the solitude of the desert – whether real or metaphorical – in order to seek God, free from the competing demands and obligations of human society. There is, not surprisingly therefore, much talk of fleeing in the literature of the desert fathers. They are constantly fleeing the world, fleeing its distractions, its unwanted attentions and sometimes even fleeing from one another. Remaining silent and withdrawing from the world can be perceived as being indifferent or irresponsible, perhaps contributing to the impression many people seem to have that religion is all about running away from life – its pressures and obligations – to seek refuge in a protective fantasy. No doubt there are some for whom religion is an escape or an excuse of one sort or another. Such people will have a worldview and identity that is hard and brittle; fiercely contested, easily shattered. But this is not a fact about religion so much as a fact about human beings, and as true of those who inhabit secular worldviews as it is of anyone else. For me religion is not about running away from life at all. If anything it is more to do with running towards the truth of who and what we really are. This would certainly be a better way of characterizing the monastic life, which represents a flight not from reality but from the unreality of our own inauthenticity. It leads to a deeper engagement with the truly real, a real that is encountered by burning away the layers of what we are not in the fire of ascetic practice. Indeed, asceticism is sometimes described as a 'fiery torch', suggesting both the heat that incinerates our impurities and the light that reveals the truth.

And yet the notion persists that being a monk or a nun is a personal, almost selfish, 'lifestyle choice' – a bit of a cushy number – even though it could not be further from the truth than to imagine that life in a monastery is all peace and harmony. From the little I know, it is definitely not an easy option to live cheek-by-jowl with a group of people you have not chosen to live with, under obedience to a discipline that compels you to stick at it whether you like it or not. Furthermore, it is absurd to assume that it is only social misfits, unable to cope with life in the 'real world', who take refuge in the cloister. Monks believe that if you are unable to get along with others, you will hardly be able to cope with living alone. Anyone who thought that joining a monastery would be a good way of escaping their problems in life would soon find that the difficulties they faced in the world were present in the monastery too, and perhaps even amplified by the absence of the usual distractions we take for granted. The truth is, we never escape from ourselves.

Monasticism is not, therefore, about escapism. On the contrary, it is everyday life that tends to be escapist. In everyday life we avoid coming to terms with our own emptiness by filling it with shopping and entertainment. Not in a monastery. You can't go out for a drink with friends when you want to unwind; nor even just relax in front of the television. And if you have an argument, you can't slam the door and walk away: you have to stay put and sort it out. By stripping away all that normally fills our everyday life and constitutes the persona we present to the world, the monastery brings us face to face with ourselves as we are. This will inevitably include some things that we might not wish to deal with. In the monastic life we see ourselves as if reflected in a mirror; a mirror that turns everything we take for granted upside down: not just for the sake of it, but in order that we may become more fully who and what we are really meant to be. None of the monks I know are taking the easy way out, or hiding from the world; rather they have deliberately chosen a different and sometimes more demanding way of being *in* the world.

The apparent contradiction between fleeing, on the one hand, and being still on the other can best be reconciled by understanding that renouncing the world does not necessarily mean running away from responsibility. Once when asked for a 'word', Macarius responded: 'Flee from men.' When asked to explain, he said that to flee 'means to sit in your cell and weep for your sins'.[127] Tears feature prominently in monastic literature, but this does not mean the early monks of Egypt had a morbid obsession with guilt; rather it means they acknowledged and faced up to that which stood between them and God – in other words, their 'sin'. This is to take responsibility for oneself, for what one has done, and therefore by extension, one's relationships with others. Paradoxically, to 'flee from men' is not to run away from the world, but to face it. In this sense, to flee is actually to be still. It is to stop the constant running away that characterizes 'normal' life; to stop indulging in the fantasies and delusions that prevent us from seeing things as they are, and ultimately, therefore, prevent us from being free. On another occasion Macarius said, 'flee, brothers'. Puzzled, they asked him what they were to flee from, given that they were already living in the desert. He put his finger to his lips and said, 'I tell you, you must flee this', before disappearing into his cell and shutting the door.[128] It is not the outer world that the monk must withdraw from, but the chattering demons of his own mind.

Monasticism contains many puzzling incongruities, one of the most marked being the very idea of a monastic *community* in the first place. Monks are, after all, by definition, solitary; but in a monastery they chose to live alone together. This tension is nowhere more apparent than in a Carthusian monastery where the brethren have

---

[127] *Alphabetical Collection* Macarius 27.
[128] *Systematic Collection* Self Control 27.

almost no contact whatsoever with the outside world, and very little contact with one another, as they spend most of their time alone in their cells. It is one of the many curious ironies of the monastic life that the most suitable arena for cultivating silence is among others. As Amma Syncletica points out, silence does not necessarily follow as a consequence of being alone: 'There are many who live in the mountains and behave as if they were in the town, and they are wasting their time. It is possible to be a solitary in one's own mind while living in a crowd, and it is possible for one who is a solitary to live in the crowd of his own thoughts.'[129] Most monks I have talked to would concur that it is not essential to join a monastery in order to do what a monk does, for we all belong to communities of one sort or another. A monastery is simply a place where the pressure of living alongside others – and doing what you have to do before what you want to do – undermines the egocentricity that comes between us and God, preventing us from being true to who and what we are really meant to be. Similar conditions prevail in a marriage, at work and so on. By living in community, the self can acquire the humility and obedience – in short, the art of listening – that both depends on, and leads to, silence.

The enclosure of the monastery imposes an outer discipline of silence, inspired by the silent emptiness of the desert, with its vast unobstructed horizons, which the early monks of Egypt understood as a symbol of the inner silence that is the deepest reality of what we are. Silence leaves us with nothing but our self: it is our basic nature, whereas what we call 'I' is but a noisy thought. Such thoughts come

---

[129] *Alphabetical Collection* Syncletica 19.

and go, but behind them there is no thinker – just being itself. And that is what we are. We have to be silent in order to hear – in order to see, in order to know – the self lying beneath the self that has been created out of all our thoughts, memories, and desires. By silencing the strident demands of the ego and withdrawing one's attention from the things that possess us, the voice of truth can be heard. This is the voice not of the self, but one fundamentally *other* than self, through which the self comes to be known as it truly is. Self-knowledge – knowing the self as nothing in itself – is at the same time also therefore a kind of self-forgetting; it occurs when we momentarily let go of all our fantasies and projections, concepts and constructs, and just quietly abide in the simple intuition of being. Silence is the necessary pre-requisite for knowledge of one's self, and therefore knowledge of God.

Silence allows us to put a little distance between ourselves and all that, quite literally, occupies our lives, our time, and our minds. To be silent is to put things into perspective. It is to let go of our needless preoccupation with the past and the future, and become aware of the still centre behind the internal commentary, allowing in turn for the possibility of an encounter with God – the reality that is what is. Just as we will not hear the birds singing outside if we have the television on, so the monk remains silent in order to listen; still in order to be present to the presence of God. By cultivating silence, we draw aside the curtain on which we project the ephemeral fantasies and obsessions of our so-called 'normal' life, a life characterized by being anywhere and indeed everywhere but here and now. To be present is not to be floating in fantasy or memory, not to be thinking happiness lies just over the horizon – if only we could change that one small detail in our present circumstances. During my stay with the Carthusians, I really noticed how most of the time we are simply not present: not even to ourselves or each other, never mind God. We encounter God – or truth if you prefer that word – in the silent emptiness that is the deepest reality of what we are, the place where, emptied of ourselves, we can participate in that in which 'we live and move and have our being'. Not that we are God, of course, but we are, ultimately, what God is.

In the desert tradition, silence is often likened to a pool of water, in which we are only able to see our reflection when its surface is completely still. 'Just as it is impossible to see one's own image in water that has been disturbed', says Evagrius, 'so too the mind will not be able to see the Lord as in a mirror [. . .] without having puri-fied the soul'.[130] This is not to say we must try and force the mind to be quiet, but rather that silence is simply a state we reach when, like a fire deprived of fuel, distractions and restlessness naturally fade away. When a desert monk complained that he could not control his wayward thoughts, his teacher answered, 'Go on sitting in your cell, and your thoughts will come back from their wanderings.'[131] In a way, then, there is nothing to achieve in prayer; we do not have to try to be quiet in order to be silent, we just have to be. Silence is a state of non-being that is being itself.

In order to hear the word of truth, we have to empty ourselves of our selves, like Christ did in giving himself to the cross. God speaks in the silence and we must be silent in order to hear his word. This is

---

[130] Evagrius, *Exhortations* 2.5.
[131] *Systematic Collection* Fortitude 30.

why it is important to realize that prayer is not so much about talking as about listening. One could even describe it as just sitting and waiting. Prayer is about cultivating a state of being open and receptive, and the necessary precondition of this receptivity is silence. We need to be quiet in order to listen. Silent prayer lies at the heart of the Christian contemplative tradition, and it has an impeccable pedigree. After all, Jesus was in the habit of withdrawing to deserted places to be alone, often spending the night in prayer on the mountainside. As well as advising us not to 'heap up empty phrases', Jesus commands us to 'pray in secret'.[132] A secret is something we keep silent about. If you say to someone, 'Can you keep a secret?' It means, 'Don't tell anyone – don't say anything about this to anyone.'

Silence and revelation thus go hand in hand; they are two sides of the same coin. We see this graphically illustrated in the Gospels. Often, when Jesus reveals his true (i.e. divine) nature – such as by means of a healing miracle – he orders the person concerned not to tell anyone about it. They must keep silence. He casts out demons, commanding them to be silent – that is, to cease to be – for their nature is chatter. He heals a leper, a deaf man, and the daughter of Jarius; in each case charging the people in question not to say anything to anyone. When Peter confesses that Jesus is the messiah, Jesus instructs the other disciples not to tell anyone about it, and at the time of his transfiguration, the disciples who are with him have an experience of God in the cloud, which renders them speechless. Once again Jesus orders them not to tell anyone what

---

[132] Matthew 6.6–7.

they have seen.[133] I take this as confirmation that silence is the only appropriate response to something awe-inspiring, like an encounter with truth. We have the same sort of experience in our own small way when we experience something of great beauty, such as a stunning view or a magnificent work of art. So if an encounter with God leads to silence, then maybe silence can lead to an encounter with God.

A leaf flutters noiselessly to the ground. Silence. Not because there is nothing we can say about it, but because there is no *it* about which there could even be anything to say in the first place.

---

[133] For healing miracles and exorcisms, see: Mark 5.43, 1.44, and 7.36. For the 'messianic secret,' see: Mark 8.29–30; and for the Transfiguration, see: Mark 9.9 (Cf. Luke 9.36 and Matthew 17.9).

CHAPTER TWELVE

Faith and Doubt

Everything seemed to be going just fine at Parkminster until a few days into the third of my four weeks. Up to this point I had been feeling strangely ambivalent about the whole thing. It was certainly proving to be an interesting and worthwhile experience in many ways: challenging because of the discipline, fulfilling on account of the opportunity to deepen my meditation practice. Yet somehow I did not feel fully engaged at a more personal level: I didn't feel I really *needed* to be there. And then one day, I suddenly experienced that profound sadness, that deep yearning I have felt many times now, and reluctantly recognize as a call to . . . a call to what exactly? The spiritual life? A life lived according to what really matters?

Yes, something like that.

It happens whenever I get a glimpse of what I know in my heart to be true, and yet which at another level I cannot or will not accept. It is as if there is a voice saying, 'Go on, you know you want to really.' Except, of course, that I don't actually hear a voice as such, I just feel the tears welling up in my eyes, and that is what they seem to be saying to me. I wish this would stop happening. I like the world. Well, sometimes at least. I take pleasure in life, I want to experience its fullness. I don't want to give it all up. I understand the rationale of renunciation, that I would not be denying myself the enjoyment of life, just giving up my claim to ownership of it. I know that ultimately there is nothing to lose and everything to gain. I know all the theory. But it still feels as if there is a price to pay, albeit for the sake of a future reward, and my faith in that clearly is not strong enough to make me take up my cross and follow the path to its logical conclusion. That is where the obstruction lies, and that is what makes me sad. I am like the rich young man of the Gospel story. Though well-intentioned and virtuous enough: he keeps the commandments, does what he is supposed to do – he is no prodigal son – nevertheless, he lacks sufficient faith to go all the way. After being told what really matters, after a glimpse of the truth revealed by Jesus, he turns away grieving, unable to give up his world. I know those tears. Like him, I do not want to give up my world either, although if I am honest, I know I have lost the taste for much of what I still cling to. So I hesitate, something holds me back. The head is saying, 'I'm only prepared to go this far', while the heart is saying, 'I want to go all the way!' Why can't I sign up for the full package, when at one level that is clearly what I really want to do?

Monasticism strikes me as being the most authentic and at the same time most artificial way of life, the most abnormal and yet the most truly normal. Of all the various ways of being in the world, it is the religious life that speaks to me with the greatest conviction. It says: 'This is what it is all about, this is what really matters.' Nothing else even comes close. In the end it is, I believe, a sure path to perfect fulfilment, but . . .

But, like the rich young man, I cannot surrender my attachments, my notions of who and what I am. I cannot let go of my self, or that in which my identity is invested – be it my intellect, desires, will or whatever – and yet ironically, I know full well that giving up the self in all these aspects is the necessary precondition for gaining the freedom I seek. 'If any want to become my followers', says Jesus, 'let them deny themselves and take up their cross and follow me. For those who want to save their life will lose it, and those who lose their life for my sake will find it'.[134] In promising the ultimate freedom Jesus demands the ultimate sacrifice – death on a cross, or laying aside the self in order to reveal God – a sacrifice often symbolized in Christian iconography by the pelican, which was believed to revive its chicks with its own blood. In some accounts, the pelican also symbolizes the hermit monk, giving up the world in order to live alone in the desert and seek God. I closed my eyes and thought hard about dying. But I still could not quite make that leap of faith – that necessary and no doubt worthwhile sacrifice of my self – trusting in what I intuitively feel must be true, yet cannot quite believe. When I put my problem to Dom Cyril he laughed and said:

"God help you!" And then he added, "You've done a dangerous thing in coming to this place!" He agreed that I was trying to be practical, looking for a reasonable way of balancing my competing desires for God and the world. It all sounded very sensible, he thought, in a very English sort of a way. But if I really wanted to resolve the matter properly, then what I needed to do was go back to the original grace, the moment of conversion, and strive to be true to that first instinct.

"Whether or not you were ready for it at the time", he said, "whatever you experienced at that point contained the sign that indicates

---

[134] Matthew 16.24–5. Cf. Matthew 10.39; Mark 8.35; Luke 9.24; John 12.25.

what you are really called to". I thought of myself sitting on the banks of the Ganges, resolving to follow the spiritual path and yes, deciding to forsake the world.

On that day I made a commitment. I embarked on a career in the religion business, and one way or another I have been doggedly pursuing it ever since. Nevertheless there is still a tension, and I expect there always will be. But that is true of any commitment. I feel it should be possible to find a balance, and yet at the same time I know that in trying, for example, to be in the world but not of the world, I am essentially seeking a compromise, and this surely cannot result in fulfilment. To attempt to satisfy both sides is to satisfy neither. It would be better to go all the way, one way or the other, than remain unfulfilled on both accounts. If I ask myself what really matters, I can unhesitatingly say: 'to seek God and to do his will'. There is no turning back once you have set foot on this path, once the seed has been sown, once you realize that the things that used to matter really do not matter any more. But – and there is always a 'but' – either it is not clear exactly how I am supposed to do this, or else I know exactly what I need to do, but am simply in denial. So what is stopping me? Attachment. My belief that I know what is what. That and a lingering fear that I will lose something by giving myself away. I just cannot take the plunge.

What I wanted back then, sitting on the banks of the Ganges, was to go all the way, to renounce the world, and commit myself wholly to God – whatever that might mean. And I did it for a couple of years. And for a couple of years I was blissfully happy. And then I got involved in all the other stuff again. But at some level I must still feel that it is what I really want. Which is why I become so melancholy when I see it because at another level I do not want to give up the world, I cannot let it go. So I cry like a little child who has been told he can't have an ice-cream. What else can I do? I cannot die to the world, but at the same time I cannot be happy in the world. So I sit on the fence, refusing to budge, unable to tell which side has the greener grass. What else can I do? Secretly hope that someone will come along and give me a push? And like the rich young man I weep because I am torn in two and it really hurts.

"If we'd had this conversation ten years ago, it might have been a different story", I said. Dom Cyril just smiled. "This is exactly what I was looking for back then. But having said that, I had to do all the things I've done in the meantime so I probably wouldn't have stuck it out. And now I'm the rich young man: my intentions are good, but I don't want to give up the world."

"Yes, it's a difficult one", he agreed, "and there are lots of people – right here around this cloister in fact – with stories just like yours". There was a long pause. "Of course, there is one way guaranteed to resolve this problem, and that's prayer. But it's risky. You have to be careful what you ask for." I waited anxiously for him to go on. "You can try praying for a contemplative vocation. But be warned, because you *will* get it, though not necessarily in the form you expect."

"I know it's what really matters, but I lack the faith necessary to . . ."

"Never mind 'but', just act as if you had it. You may be surprised at the result."

Faith is often caricatured as believing in things that are not true – or at least, that cannot be proven. But maybe Dom Cyril was right. Maybe faith means acting *as if* something were true. For me, the important questions to ask when talking about religion are not necessarily 'is it true?' but rather 'what does it mean?' and 'what would be the effect of living life *as if* it were true?' Thus, when I say 'I believe' in something, I am not asserting that something is true – if that entails a proposition corresponding to an empirically verifiable fact about the objective world. Rather, to say 'I believe' is to say that something is meaningful to me in terms of a particular context. Neither faith itself, nor the beliefs that constitute it – those specific propositions that make up a worldview – have anything to do with truth, as that word is usually understood. Not because those beliefs are false, in comparison with some other set of propositions that are true, but because truth itself turns out to be much more interesting than commonly supposed. This is due in no small part to the fact that whatever we call truth must inevitably rest on foundational assumptions or dogmas – of which we are for the most part not even aware – that have to be accepted as given, on faith.

Therefore the question we ought to be asking is not whether something is true, but rather what purpose does it serve to tell such a story and live by it? Faith is not something that can be observed and measured; it has to be lived and experienced. Faith is an expression of trust: it does not pertain to matters of fact but the mysterious and unknown. You have to enter into faith, at least partly blind, knowing that you cannot know. That is simply what trust entails. An oft-repeated mistake, common to both religious and non-religious people alike, is to think that faith implies a closed book, that to be religious is to be someone who insists they have all the answers, whereas in fact, it is to be someone who is asking the questions. Faith is the journey, not the destination; a series of open questions rather than a set of fixed answers. This is why faith and doubt are not mutually exclusive but mutually dependent: they co-exist. The absence of doubt would be a state of certainty, but if I had all the answers I would not need faith: I would know it all already.

To be asking questions, then, is the first step of faith. The second is to believe, on trust, that in spite of appearances to the contrary, life does in fact have a meaning and a purpose after all. People complain that religion is nonsense. In some ways they might be right. But it is also true that nonsense is what you would be left with in a world without any religion whatsoever, because a religion is by definition what we call our effort to make sense out of nonsense. Indeed, it is precisely because there are no answers, no intrinsic meaning and purpose, that we have to supply it ourselves. This is why the tenets of faith so often seem to contradict what we know from experience. Indeed, that is the whole point: faith is a story we tell ourselves that contradicts the facts, thus enabling us to rationalize the uncertainty and absurdity of existence. And this reveals a deeper truth: faith is the basis of reason itself, because fundamental axioms of some sort have to be assumed in order to be able to think at all.

The word 'God' is one such foundational assumption. We may wish to say that we have 'no need of that hypothesis', but getting rid of God only means we will need some other word that performs the same function in whatever other sentences we use to construct the world. Try explaining anything without first assuming a set of primary axioms. If you think the word God is meaningless, how about Truth, Reality, Goodness, Beauty, Rights or Love? Is the existence of the 'things' these words refer to any easier to prove? Can we even talk about them in the first place without at the same time assuming an absolute ground or authority to guarantee their validity? 'God' is the object of faith in the sense of being the word we use to provide our horizon of meaning; more than just a 'useful fiction', it is a pragmatic necessity. Thus faith is intrinsic to being human, an irreducible fact about what we are and how we work, something true about us, whether one is explicitly 'religious' or not.

Whatever the word 'truth' refers to, it is ultimately a mystery, something hidden, like a face that cannot see itself; just as although we may know *that* reality is, we know not *what* it is. Because it is everything. And nothing. In the meantime, and for all practical purposes, what we say is or is not true is determined by the story: absolute within it, but relative to the conditions that define it. It is very hard to see this, because it requires a fundamental switch in the way we are conditioned from birth to perceive the world. So for example, we blindly assume that the objects referred to by language exist independently of the language used to talk about them, and that our beliefs can be judged according to whether or not they correspond to a state of affairs in the 'objective' world. But our beliefs, whatever they may be – 'religious' or otherwise – do not derive from facts so much as define them; they are not statements about the world so much as the underlying grammar of the story through which the world is experienced.

'But if it's only a story', you may be thinking, 'does that mean it's not true?' This question is based on a fundamental misunderstanding: the notion that we can adopt an objective stance somewhere outside the story, when in fact we are characters within it. To ask which story is *really* true is to miss the point, because different stories serve different purposes; in absolute terms one story is as good as another, and all stories have the same truth status. In the meantime, in life as in literature, I would like to think that some stories are 'better' than others. Some stories are deemed to be more coherent, well-structured or useful than others. Some stories can be said to be more 'fit for purpose'. Some – if lived – seem to result in more fulfilled and fulfilling lives. And this is the key point: a story alone is not sufficient, it needs to be connected with a practice. Indeed, it needs to be the story *of* a practice – and our practice needs to be the practise of a story – we need both together, making an integrated whole. Our actions and experiences are good and true in as much as they measure up to the story, and the story is good and true in as much as it proves to be so over time and in a wide variety of contexts. We could specify further criteria, such as that the purpose of our story should be transformative and redemptive, and that it should affirm the intrinsic value of being human, or if you prefer, the 'divinity' of humanity. In this sense, an actual religion – as opposed to a story with religious elements – offers a unified and fully resolved story in which everything is part of a comprehensive picture of who we are, why we are here and what we are supposed to do about it. A 'good' story, then, is one with a plot that adds up.

The 'implicit theology' underlying our secular reality-ordering narratives, by contrast, is rarely quite so coherent. Worldviews based on scientific materialism, or a political ideology, may offer some answers to some of the 'big questions' traditionally reserved to religion, but they do not on the whole provide any corresponding basis for our moral conduct. For example, the notion of the 'survival of the fittest' serves as an excellent explanatory model in many contexts, but the consequences of taking it as an ethical maxim would be catastrophic: society as we know it would cease to exist. These days, however, fewer and fewer people are prepared to buy into the old stories – which are increasingly in danger of being forgotten. Yet at the same time, they show no sign of being able to get by without stories of some sort. The fact is that modern, supposedly secular, societies have neither outgrown nor dispensed with religion. Far from it. They have just given the temple a makeover and renamed it 'The Mall'. God is dead, long live God!

Lots of people say they believe in God, and are interested in spirituality (for a variety of not always very spiritual reasons), but they do not go to church because they cannot believe in, let's say, the Creeds. They either reject what they naively call 'dogma' – as if their own beliefs were not similarly founded on taken-for-granted assumptions – or else excuse themselves on the basis that it would be insincere to stand up in church and recite statements whose literal content they felt unable to affirm. First of all, this is to see religious truth in narrowly literalistic terms; at a deeper level, it misses the point entirely. Often, what has happened is that a childish form of religion has – quite rightly – been rejected, only to be replaced with an equally simplistic belief system, misleadingly called 'rationality'. It is not that religion is neither useful nor true, but that as a culture we have lost the vocabulary of faith, and are fast losing any ability to use our imagination. The varieties of fundamentalism, both religious and secular, currently in vogue have this much in common: they rely on a one-dimensional account of truth and demonstrate an apparent inability to engage imaginatively with reality. Furthermore, just as our basic physical needs have remained largely unchanged since the dawn of time – though the means by which we satisfy them may have changed considerably – so the same applies to our basic spiritual needs. They remain in need of fulfilment, one way or another. This explains why it is that many people actually *want* religion; the problem is they cannot find the religion they want. Sometimes religious institutions are at fault here; they really are meaningless and irrelevant. But as often this attitude says more about us than it does about religion.

Our yearning for a sense of meaning and personal fulfilment has become increasingly associated with the now widely held view that one can transact a personal relationship with the divine, independently of participation in any particular religious tradition. Moreover, 'organized religion' is often seen as the enemy of 'true spirituality'. Apparently one does not need to go to church to be 'spiritual', or even – for that matter – to be a Christian. Evagrius would no doubt identify this as yet another manifestation of the demon of acedia, which makes us think that 'pleasing the Lord is not a question of being in a particular place: for scripture says that the divinity can be worshipped anywhere'.[135] As it happens, the desert fathers probably did not go to church very often either. Although the brethren gathered for communal prayers, priests were evidently regarded with deep suspicion, and it would appear that some monks may have conducted their spiritual lives entirely outside the structures of the institutional church. There are, however, important differences between them and us. The desert fathers may have been wary of 'priestcraft' but they were unswerving in their devotion to God and deeply committed to the life of faith – and all that went with it. For

---

[135] Evagrius, *Praktikos* 12.

us, on the other hand, it is commitment itself that seems to be the fundamental problem.

We are all consumers now, and expect the world to conform to our requirements. Religion has traditionally demanded the opposite: that we submit to the possibility of being changed. This is the real issue underlying our rejection of whatever it is we say we do not like about church. We are put off by the fact that it is hard work, and requires commitment. The desert fathers, by contrast, *expected* the spiritual life to be arduous. Abba Poemen said: 'Brothers, is it not in order to endure affliction that we have come to this place? But now there is no affliction for us here. So I am getting my sheepskin ready to go where there is some affliction and there I shall find peace.'[136] We have no problem with the idea that physical training is strenuous; in fact we would feel cheated if it was not. So why should spiritual training be any different? Just opting for what suits us is never going to change us. With this in mind I suggest that what we don't like about 'organized religion' should be seen in a different light, as grist to the mill, something to engage with. Strange as it may initially seem, there is actually something rather healthy about the act of just standing up in public and reciting liturgical formulae – *especially* if one does not fully understand or subscribe to the literal content of every phrase. It is an act that symbolically says, 'I am not in charge here, I don't know everything.' Indeed, contrary to the fantasy that all will be revealed by 'progress', it is more likely that humanity will not, indeed *cannot* ever know everything. Being human is a fundamental mystery: there is no complete and perfect

---

[136] *Alphabetical Collection* Poemen 44.

explanation – of anything – that is absolutely true. Having the humility and self-awareness to acknowledge this from time to time would surely not be a bad thing.

The 'problem' of organized religion – not that there could be any other kind of course – is not that it is sterile, boring, or irrelevant but that we have become so arrogant. As a culture we have lost our sense of accountability before God, before nature, and before each other. Therefore, reciting the Creeds, or indeed participating in any other aspect of sacred ritual, is not primarily about those propositional statements and what they ostensibly refer to but rather what the act of doing it means; the literal content of the words we utter is the least significant aspect of prayer. We may think that we need or ought to understand why we do something before we agree to do it, but in fact there are many instances in life where it is the other way around, where it is necessary to do something first in order to come to an understanding of why we do it, or what it means. Children, for example, learn to do things long before they are given to comprehend the reasons why. Their parents will tell them 'Just do it!' Only later will they learn to formulate an explanatory story. Going to church is similar. A religion is not simply a check-list of beliefs, but a practice; a way of life as much as an ideology, which has to be practised and lived in order to be understood.

Whether we claim to have a religion or not, we all believe in all sorts of stories based on foundations that have an essentially religious character, for they have to be taken as given. Many of our supposedly secular assumptions are implicitly, and often inversely, theological; outcomes of largely unchanged religious ways of thinking. Indeed, there is no other way it could be: all our story-telling has a religious character because that is, by definition, the nature of stories – they convey meaning – and telling stories is something people do simply by virtue of being human beings, endowed as we are with self-awareness. To those who complain that none of these stories are actually true – that there is no way things really are, no grand narrative, no meaning or purpose – I would suggest that this only reinforces how necessary our stories really are. In other words, it is precisely *because* there may be no ultimate truth that we need and have stories that give us meaning and purpose where otherwise there would be neither.

To be human is to live by a story. It is my conviction that the monastic life embodies one of the most explicit and coherent demonstrations of this fact. Unfortunately however, I suspect that the majority of people would regard monasticism as a highly specialized vocation, reserved only for an ever decreasing minority. This could not be further from the truth. There is a monk within us all, and in the monastic life there is an example we can all follow, in some way or other. Admittedly, this may not seem obvious at first, but like the story itself – indeed, like life itself – monasticism is full of paradoxes: freedom depends on obedience, self-knowledge is knowledge of others, and we have to lose our life in order to find it. At one level, these contradictions suggest a goal that is impossible to attain. But this does not mean that the goal – the goal of life lived authentically, true to who and what we are really meant to be – is not worth striving for, for it is in that striving that we become more than what we are.

POSTSCRIPT

February 10, 2006. Early afternoon. It was sunny, mild for the time of year, and I was walking along a beach on the Dorset coast, watching the waves fold onto the pebbly shore before being sucked back out to sea again. A phone call from the bishop to say I had been recommended to train for the priesthood. Twelve years to the day since having my last gin and tonic on a plane to India. Feelings of joy, feelings of dread. During my first week at seminary, the story of the rich young man was read in chapel. This time, however, I was glad to hear it.

I have often been asked why I want to be a priest. It's a good question, and I don't claim to have all the answers. But there are two important facts about life that I find hard to ignore. The first is that religion – in some form – like art or politics, is intrinsic to being human. Simply put, religion represents that area of human experience pertaining to matters of ultimate concern. The existential 'big questions', such as, who are we? why are we here? and what are we supposed to do about it? do not – indeed cannot – have factual answers. No less worthy of being asked as a result of that, they are just different from other types of question. They do not have answers that are true or false in any simplistic way because they are questions of meaning, questions whose answers are not facts but stories – the stories by which we live our lives.

The second is that any and every human community includes within it some who are 'set apart' as ministers or priests, to be providers of spiritual services, or simply to be there – in whatever way is needed. For such people, a religious commitment is not just a part of their life but the whole of it: like an artist, what they do is what they are. In any society, the minister of religion is someone with a publicly sanctioned responsibility to pray for and on behalf of the people, a moral duty to speak out in the name of righteousness and truth, and a mission to engage with individuals at the existential level. Somewhat like the poet or the artist, the priest's role is to act as a mediator between us and whatever it is that provides the transcendent meaning-giving horizon of our earthly existence. They represent us to God, and God to us. To put it another way, their job is to manage the myth of our lives, helping us to put our personal story into the context of a bigger story, one that makes life meaningful and which may – if lived faithfully – prove to be transformative.

And finally, I simply accept the fact that that is who and what I am.